D0476096

THE EXCITEMENT OF WRITING

THE EXCITEMENT OF WRITING

Edited by

A. B. CLEGG

Chief Education Officer
West Riding of Yorkshire

1965

CHATTO & WINDUS
LONDON

Published by
Chatto & Windus (Educational) Ltd
42 William IV Street
London W.C.2

•

Clarke, Irwin & Co. Ltd
Toronto

First published in this edition June 1964
Second Impression October 1964
Third Impression March 1965
Fourth Impression November 1965

© County Council of the
West Riding of Yorkshire, 1964

Printed in Great Britain by
Chorley & Pickersgill Ltd
Leeds

"YOUNG RHETORIC"

"... But the English pupil is distrusted if he or she includes in an essay words outside the drabbest lingo of use and wont. The English must keep their style from any proximity to a purple patch and reduce their prose to the melancholy monotony of a khaki uniform. The examiner will expect the candidates to have read the English authors who poured out the colour and music of the language; but he will drop heavily on any who think this a reason for dipping their pens in the inks of scarlet and blue . . ."

Extract from a leader in *The Times*, 13th May, 1963.

FOREWORD

BY DENYS THOMPSON

The core of this book is an anthology of children's writing. However, its quite distinctive character rests not only in the examples collected, but in the accounts of the circumstances in which the writing was produced, in the implications for the content and method of teaching English and in the short route to certain conclusions about external examinations and their ancillary text-books.

It was produced earlier this year by the Education Department of the West Riding of Yorkshire. The Education Officer, Mr A. B. Clegg, noted that "Each year schools of all kinds spend at least many hundreds of thousands of pounds ... on books of English exercises designed to prepare pupils for external examinations such as the Eleven Plus selection test, the 'o' and 'A' levels of the G.C.E, and even for examinations not yet fully operative such as the 'Use of English' paper ... and the Certificate of Secondary Education." And in a survey of writing in schools it was found that schools producing the most sensitive work not only did not use these books of exercises but in many cases considered their use to be harmful. As a result, the work set out in Chapter III was collected from two Infant, ten Junior, two Modern and two Grammar Schools, ten of them in small and sometimes extremely depressing mining communities, and a privately printed edition of the present book was circulated to West Riding schools.

On the evidence from his schools, the editor quickly disposes of the belief that the best way to improve a child's power of expression is to work through exercises, and goes on to make the very important point that "the ability to use words well is an indivisible achievement which once learned will be used effectively in whatever kind of writing the child does". This is demonstrated, strikingly and cogently, in pages 10–16, from which it emerges quite clearly that "creative" writing in schools is neither a luxury allowed by indulgent teachers, nor a form of psychotherapy, but a mode of expression that children practise readily, deriving confidence and fluency from it, and stocking up for their "recording" work when it is called for in history, science and so on. An improvement in one kind of writing means advance all along the line.

That the children's work is good goes almost without saying; a great deal of such writing can emanate from any sound school. Once again in reading it one is moved by the vitality, the enviable sharpness of perception, an almost Elizabethan immediacy of feeling and sensation — the boy quoted on page 111 reads almost like Nashe. The older children (i.e. in double figures) often write better for their reading, as in "Rain" on page 60, to pick at random an example of what might so easily (in the wrong kind of literary environment) have slipped over the edge into falseness and affectation. But the editor (page 133) and his teachers are well aware of the dangers of quick results and over-stimulation.

Particularly interesting, especially to those who teach, are the brief introductions supplied by teachers to the selections from their schools. They should help anyone who wishes to create conditions that favour good writing. Were one to cull from these introductions a scheme of advice to young teachers on how to encourage good writing, the precepts would not be new, but of the sound and practical kind made familiar by the writings of (for example) Dr Gurrey and Mr J. H. Walsh. The making of such a scheme would incidentally be an exercise well worth carrying out by teachers-in-training. Here are some examples of the hints and ideas that emerge — story-writing at the start as an aid to fluency and good sense; continuous composition; providing incentives; the need for encouragement, not criticism; helping pupils to sincerity rather than superficial brilliance; correction and criticism by fellow-pupils as a means of vigorous improvement; writing verse, but no rhymes or metrical schemes; reading as the road to good spelling and punctuation; and the futility of books of exercises.

Exercises and drills seem to be anathema to all the schools that contribute examples, and as they are a product of mass-testing the case against external examinations starts to mount. This case is powerfully developed in Chapters V and VI; the criticisms made are all the more devastating for the fresh approach and the well-chosen examples. And how badly they are needed! We ourselves are all so much products of the system that the impact of the truth is blunted — the truth that examinations have distorted most of the subjects, from English to Physics, that they touch.

There may be some subjects, such as Languages and Mathematics, in which there is an accepted and readily tested content, that are comparatively unaffected by examining. But with English there is no content, and what matters — a sensitive response to literature and life — cannot be tested by a mass-examination. So a bogus and alien content is invented and foisted on English — so alien that it would be much better if

'O' level language tests were replaced by a foreign language. What do lend themselves to testing are knowledge of and some skill in grammar, punctuation, syntax, spelling, clause-analysis, vocabulary, précis, detecting errors ... As aids to reading and writing most of them are irrelevant and useless, and they squeeze out the living reading and writing that constitute any worthy course in English. How irrelevant and useless they are is brought home by a glance at some of the hundreds of African 'O' level scripts that litter a house in which I have been staying. Scores of the writers were 95 per cent accurate on grammar, without being able to understand or write much more than pidgin English.

As soon as an examination comes into being, teachers naturally start preparing their pupils to pass it; and it could hardly be otherwise when so much depends (in Mr Leavis's phrase) on a "stand-and-deliver" procedure. They will tend to devote most of their teaching time to such preparation, however uneducational it may be. The staple of their teaching may even consist of past examination papers; and they will almost certainly resort to text-books that never lose the smell of the examination room. Thus a method of testing what examiners deem to be useful — or examinable — becomes a full-time method of teaching; and teachers inflict on their pupils lessons that would never take place but for the demands of testing, with a content markable on a mass scale at speed and with a sort of efficiency. If they are to teach anything that promotes growth of mind and spirit, they will need cunning and strength of purpose. After an exam-warped education too many children leave school unaware of and uninterested in their own literature, to become ready customers of the entertainment industry.

Examinations are sacred cows and cannot all be got rid of at once. But the system can be rendered more tolerable, and Mr Clegg's book shows why and how. There can be enlightened syllabuses and less idiotic tests. The c.s.e. examination need not repeat the history of g.c.e. if there is variety from year to year and region to region. Determined teachers have many of them always known that to prepare for some of the papers set is not the best way of securing passes. It is a fallacy that what can be learned can and must be taught. Mechanical accuracy in the writing of English, for example, will come or will not come, with maturity, and there is very little that teacher or text-book can do about it. If there is a recipe, it consists of plentiful reading and writing — and this is no longer a pious hope, an impression from experience, but a fact proved by research. It is likely that more research will show that anything worth testing in the use of English comes most surely as a by-product.

This is a timely and salutary book, revolutionary in its implications for the teaching of English. Payers of rates and taxes should note that large sums are spent on text-books that seem to leave pupils the worse for using them. The general reader may learn from it how it is that English as the tool for nearly every subject is nowadays so often inefficient. Teachers of English and in training may see in it a means of shedding a useless load that has frustrated so much of their labour. I am sure that all who read it will be grateful to Mr Clegg and to the teachers of the West Riding for producing it.

DENYS THOMPSON

CONTENTS

B

PREFACE

This book is intended to illustrate some of the work in written English now being done in West Riding schools. It also points to some of the pressures which teachers must resist if they are to succeed with work of this kind. The book is in the main concerned with work from Junior schools, the age-group which has made the greatest progress in recent years in this County. Work from Secondary Modern and Grammar schools has also been included, as it is on these schools that some of the pressures in the form of exercises and examinations bear most hardly.

A. B. CLEGG
Chief Education Officer

Chapter I

INTRODUCTION

A minority of pupils in the schools of this country are born into families whose members speak the normal language of educated society. If a child born into such a family "picks up" any phrase which does not conform to the convention, vigorous pressures are brought to bear to make him "drop it". Such a child will go to school knowing no other forms of language than those which his teachers themselves use and which his examiners will demand of him.

There are, however, other children, possibly a majority in the country as a whole and certainly a majority in industrial areas, who have to learn this acceptable language at school but who, in some cases, may well face discouragement, or even derision, if they venture to use it at home.

For such children many social pressures inside the school and all outside it contrive to blunt the main tool of learning.

The following sentences are taken from a short statement* about these pressures and their effect on speech and writing by a boy in his first year in the sixth form of a South Yorkshire Grammar school.

> "The problem of speech facing a sixth former in a working class area is only a relatively minor one. It is a reflection of the much greater complexities he faces in having to live two lives, but his speech may be the most prominent manifestation of his embarrassment and discomfort . . .
>
> As the sixth former becomes increasingly conscious of his inadequate vocabulary, lack of fluency and lazy, slovenly

---

* The statement by this pupil is one that may be of interest to teachers generally and it is reproduced in full in an Appendix on page 136.

speech (accent is unimportant), he may attempt to do something about it, but his normal social environment is not conducive to good speech nor to the standard of social etiquette he is expected to acquire. Moreover, the effect of his trying to speak 'the Queen's English' may be ludicrous and create the wrong impression. When speaking in his usual surroundings too he may be ridiculed and he feels that he is despised.

. . . 'to get on' means interviews, speeches and many social occasions which demand well-bred manners, social ease and good speech. In order to avoid 'sitting still with thumb in mouth and fumbling fingers' at his university interview he may eventually decide to make a concerted effort to be master in his own house and to correct his speech. Such a course frequently causes friction in his family and amongst acquaintances when he finds himself inadvertently correcting their speech. As he becomes a better speaker he becomes increasingly annoyed at those who don't. Education in general has made him incompatible with working-class life."

Whatever one thinks of these statements, they are likely to leave a valid impression that speech and language for many children can be a matter of the greatest concern and can become an educational problem of major significance. How is this problem solved in the schools?

One of the most usual ways of solving this is to require pupils to work books of exercises at home and at school. These books are produced in hundreds and sold in hundreds of thousands of copies. Those that are used in schools are produced under such titles as "English Progress Papers", "The Eleven Plus Preparation Book", "Scholarship Tests as They are Set", and "The Academy G.C.E. Model Answers". Those sold for use in the home have titles such as "The Eleven Plus Home Tutor" and "The Scholarship Home Tutor and Examination Aid".

It is the purpose of this book to persuade *all* teachers to consider whether the working of exercises such as are to be found in these books is the best way of teaching children to write fluently, easily and with power.

The point about which there can be no shadow of doubt is that the working of books of exercises is the prevailing method and on it vast sums of money are spent. The sales from the County Supplies Department are evidence of this, and the books are possibly used as extensively in many homes as in schools.

Recently a number of Divisional Education Officers were asked to go to their local bookshops or newsagents and ask for books of English exercises which would help a child "through the scholarship", and large numbers of examples poured into the County Hall from all over the County. The booksellers of the larger towns stock a wide range of these and even the stationers in the smaller towns have their favoured publications.

In one of the much smaller communities a County Council Inspector asked at the papershop if he could buy such a book and he was told "No, we don't stock them, when our Ian took it we had to send away for a copy".

In another very small town a Headmistress who makes no use of such exercises asked for a book of them and was told "No, we don't stock them but you can get them at so-and-so" (naming a well-known chain store). She was given a list of titles. (The Education Officer even secured a bottle of 11+ mixture produced by a reputable firm of druggists.)

Yet there are schools which make little or no use of the output of this immense industry and indeed it is certainly true to say that at the present time a significant revolution in English teaching, which has little use for exercises, is taking place and it is similar in pattern and intention to that in Art and Movement which in recent years, particularly in the Junior schools, has done so much to enrich the child's experience and increase his will to learn.

This change in English teaching in Junior schools has been brought about by a number of gifted and determined teachers who have rejected the examination approach to English teaching with its attendant exercises and are developing power and fluency of writing by encouraging children to enjoy the use of words as they have been brought to enjoy the discriminating use of colour in their painting or of expressive movement in their Dance and Drama.

There are set out in the pages which follow a number of pieces of children's writing taken from schools which are deliberately encouraging each child to draw sensitively on his own store of words and to delight in setting down his own ideas in a way which is personal to him and stimulating to those who read what he has written.

As the purpose of this collection of work is to focus attention on the child's powers of expression rather than the technical accomplishments of writing, spelling and punctuation, some of the spelling in the examples of Infant work has been corrected. In most of the Junior school work, however, spelling and punctuation stands as it was written.

The work from each school is prefaced by a statement from the teacher responsible for the children who produced it. The pieces of work have been chosen because of their freshness and power of expression, the discriminating choice of words and phrases, and the sincerity of feeling which is apparent in them.

The following chapter illustrates the two main kinds of English writing produced in our schools and the uses made of them.

Chapter II

"PENNY PLAIN AND TWOPENCE COLOURED"

It is sometimes held that a pupil's ability to use words well does not apply generally to all his work and that if he writes poetry or expressive prose really well it does not follow that he will be able to give a clear account of a scientific experiment. It is no doubt this contention which gives rise to the belief that the best way to achieve clarity and conciseness of expression is to compel the pupil to work through exercises designed to this end and that the poorer his ability the more exercises he will need to do.

All the evidence which has been received from the schools of the County at every stage from the Infant school to the sixth form leads to the belief that this contention is in the main false and that the ability to use words well is an indivisible achievement which once learned will be used effectively in whatever kind of writing the child does, though this does not of course alter the fact that the boy's interests will lead him more in one direction than in another.

In order to examine this very important point of teaching, it may be helpful arbitrarily to divide the pupil's written English into two categories, which for purposes of this discussion we may call his "personal" English and his "recording" English. In this context the word "personal" is used to describe the English which a pupil would use when writing poetry or expressive prose, or when writing about his personal experiences, impressions or imaginings, relying on his own store of words to do so.

His "recording" English, which may make up nine-tenths of his writing in school, he will use for his History, his Geography, Science, Religious Instruction, and so on. Many of the words and phrases that he uses will be taken not from his own store but from books recently read or notes recently taken down. As children grow older this kind of writing becomes increasingly important as it includes the power to adduce evidence and set out a logical argument.

The following passages illustrate these two kinds of writing. The first four are typical examples of English used for recording.

An 11-year-old records what she has observed and learned about a chestnut twig.

"A horse chestnut twig is completely covered with a corky bark in which are many lenticels through which air goes in and out. On the buds are sticky scale leaves. These leaves are sticky so that no insect can destroy them and the developing leaves and flower. Inside the scale leaves are the green leaves which are only sticky at the top. Inside these are the developing leaves. These are furry. They form a circle covered at the top. Inside is the developing flower. There are three different types of scars. One is a horseshoe shaped leaf scar. This is formed by a leaf falling off. In spring scale leaves fall off the bud leaving a girdle scar. The third is a flower scar called a saddle scar. On the horseshoe scar are little holes. These are the veins.

In spring food and water travel up the twig and the scale leaves peel down with the warmth. The scale leaves leave a girdle scar. The growing leaves have white hairs on them. When the leaves have expanded these white hairs drop off. Also the twig grows. These leaves have the sun shining on them and they make food."

A 14-year-old Modern school pupil in an examination records what she has learned about a tapeworm.

"A tapeworm is an example of a parasite. It is so called because it is a flat organism and looks like a piece of tape. It feeds on a host and without this it cannot survive. Its host is man. It lives in the duodenum, the first part of the small intestine. It attaches itself by hooks. It has many segments called proglottids. They are smaller nearer the anterior end and grow larger towards the posterior end. Every segment has both male and female reproductive organs but it is only the last segments which are mature and only these can reproduce."

A 14-year-old pupil in a Grammar school records a statement about the manufacture of coal-gas.

"Coal-gas is made by the destructive distillation of coal from a retort. Destructive distillation means that the products cannot be converted into coal again by allowing them to cool. The coal is heated in a vertical retort which is heated by producer-gas. A vertical retort is used because it gives more uniform heating. On the inside, gas carbon is left as a hard crust. The gas from the retort then travels through a pipe. It then passes through the hydraulic main which runs the length of the retorts and collects the materials which first condense. These are coal-tar and water. The gas then passes on to the tar well. This contains the tar from which many products can be obtained, benzene, aniline, phenol, naphthalene and others."

A sixth-former begins to record a statement on the policies of Philip II.

"Philip II came to the throne in 1556, the time which was the 'golden age' of Spain. Spanish literature was flourishing; Cervantes published his 'Don Quixote' illustrating vividly Spanish life and character. Work in history, geography, physics and mathematics was advanced. There were twenty-nine universities where the intelligence of the many Jesuits had a stimulating effect. The theatre was thriving; El Greco was beginning his work. Spain's possessions stretched from the New World, to North Africa, to Milan, to Portugal, to Franche Conte, to the Netherlands, to the Kingdom of the Two Sicilies, to the Balearic Isles and Sardinia, to Portugal and to Spain itself.

From the outset, however, there were disadvantages. 'God, Gold and Glory' were attracting some of the best men away from Spain to the New World. Gold was so easily obtainable that no real economic policy was developed. There was no intellectual freedom, so in certain aspects Spain dropped behind the rest of Europe."

In the four examples which follow pupils of different ages and different school backgrounds have used their personal vocabulary to write something which is individual and peculiarly theirs.

An infant of six embroiders a personal experience.

"One day when I came home I started to akt daft with the dog We played in the room and tinker my pet dog jumped up at me and shuved me towards the side board and when I hit the side board my haed hit the vase the best vase and it fell on my head and it fell of my head and it smashed on the floor. Well there was me sitting in the middle of bits and pieces with a large bump on my head I didnt know wot to do so I got some glue and started to put it back to pieces agian and the vas had cracks in it and I thought if I should ever be found out and then in came my mummy and daddy I heard mummy say I think I shall go and look at my best vars, then I rushed upstairs and hid under the bed and when she saw it she played hell and I felt licke a roast egg and I was full of pity I was that."

A ten-year-old boy writes of his visit to a pond.

"The wind blew the rushes very steadily and the puffy feathers on the swans' back billowed out slightly. The pond lay still and calm and looked as though it had a thin covering of ice upon it as the sun glistened on it. Shadows of the swans' beaks and necks hung like hooks in the water as the swans cut like knives through the still pond leaving a trail of bubbles behind them. Other swans stood as still as statues on the little island in the middle of the pond. They ruffled up their feathers and spread out their wings like someone just getting out of bed and stretching, getting ready to go for a swim in the calm water."

A fifteen-year-old boy in a Day Continuation school, despite his grammatical difficulties, writes powerfully of what is obviously a deeply felt personal relationship.

"In my opinion, the most interesting person in our street is a coal miner. This man is about thirty-four years old and is as fit as a fiddle. He has lived a very enjoyable life so far and I hope he will live very many more.

When 'Geoff' was a boy he was raised in a poor home, his father too was a miner, and was on the dole because of pit strikes. Every day Geoff would go to school and study hard; living only on what he could scrape, he was the oldest boy of the family and proved his worth. His was the task of house cleaning and washing at night time, whilst his mother was at the munition works, and he got no time for playing. Yet at school he proved himself in games, because he captained the senior boys football team in clogs at one game, because he had his boots stolen and his family could not afford him another pair.

At the age of fourteen he left school and went to work for the coal board as an apprentice fitter, but his father reluctantly had to take him off the job because of the small wage. Geoff then went into the mine and worked on the face. When he was seventeen he went into the Royal Navy and served a distinguished service therin. When he left the Navy, Geoff once more returned to the mine; but not on two days a week on full time, he went cutting and started to earn full money, he decided to get married and married a charming girl, who is now a loveable but sick mother.

Geoff brought up three children one boy and two girls. He treats them well and supplies all their needs, all times he is an interesting person, and I should know for I am his son."

A sixth-form girl writes of her personal reactions to a rat.

"A shadow darts across the creaky floor:
It is yours,
You menace.

Your long, sly, pointed head
Peers at me from behind a ball of rotting straw.
How I detest you!

Why do you seem to sneer?
I, afraid of you!

You crouch there,
Your teeth like tiny chisels
Waiting to sink into my flesh.

I stare at you, pretending I feel no fear,
Whilst you, hypocrite,
Return the same stare.

Why do you glare at me
With such large and crafty eyes,
Hypnotist?

You move,
My blood turns cold.
What! Am I a man or a mouse?"

Much of this book will be devoted to the "personal" writing of children in the belief that those pupils whose personal writing is maintained at a high standard throughout their school life will tend to write well whatever they write. There may be some who doubt this and, to help them over their doubts, the next few pages contain pieces of written work set out in contrasting pairs, each pair having been written by the same child.

A ten-year-old boy who wrote this at the beginning of his personal description of a stoat —

> "Needle-like fangs are enclosed in a snarling vicious mouth. This ferocious enemy is unwanted by many a hen, rabbit and mouse. Ready to pounce on an unwary animal. offering a challenge to all his foes. Only swiftness and bite lie between him and starvation. His back is arched in fury. Forelegs are stiff, hind legs bent and ready to pounce, tail low and curved. Tinted brown and grey, not at all like his pure white winter coat. His black shiny eyes glint evilly. Grey whiskers streak backwards, like his stroked fur. Brown, tan, fawn and nut-brown are also colours in his summer coat. How delicate and innocent the teeth may seem, but once they sank into the flesh of a frightened animal. The tiny paws with tooth-pick claws, once carried a living stoat over the countryside."

wrote this as the beginning of what he had learned at second-hand about ships —

> "The earliest boats were made by the cavemen. They cut down with their stone axes trees, which they hollowed out. These boats were an early form of the dug-out canoe. Later in the Bronze Age, men made basketwork boats, covered with skin, called coracles. The boats were light enough to be carried on men's backs, and are still used in Wales. The Phoenicians built galleys, made of wood. The ships were manned by galley slaves and used for trading. They had one to three rows of oars on each side of the ship . . ."

Another ten-year-old boy who had visited a power station wrote this from his first-hand experience about a furnace which he saw —

> "Like the wiggles on a radar screen, the lines of the vast furnace, appeared to my astonished eyes. Each wavy line

varied, all numerous shades of white, fighting as if in a battle, emerging to a valiant victory. A great fire has erupted, and along come the firemen, their armour shining bright, and each with an extinguisher. The oil heated furnace appears to be the water gushing out, endeavouring to rid the dominating flames. The thick walls surrounding these fierce wonders protect us from death. To watch is like being taken into a trance, into the world of unbelievable happenings. Just as if I was stepping into a blanket of hanging mist, while as I emerged, it began to whirl around me, it was like being taken into a world of the lost. Such a nightmare I have to leave, scarred by such torture. The shield protecting my face seems to be as though I were at a hospital, stretching to see a friend over a huge door. The stone is replaced, no longer are the furnace flames white, but a ferocious red. Fighting with all their might, threatening all his victims. Such magnificent beauty would enchant anyone who had the chance of peering into the furnace."

The same boy learned from his reading about the gunpowder plot and wrote this —

"In 1604 five Roman Catholics met in a house to talk about their King. The men decided that they should make a plot, to blow up Parliament. The plot was that one of the men should hide under the Houses of Parliament and should ignite some gunpowder to kill the King and Lords. The plotters needed plenty of money to complete their plan. They each went to different parts of England, persuaded rich gentlemen to give them money. By this time thirteen people knew of the plot, including a brave soldier who was forced to go and fight in the Spanish Army. His name was Guy Fawkes who was born at York in 1570. Guy was asked to play an important part in the plot, Guy dressed up as a servant and found out about secret meetings. The plotters set to work digging under the ground near the

Houses of Parliament. One day the men heard a noise, Guy was sent to investigate, and came back and told them it was only a coal merchant. Catesby decided to hire the merchants cellar, the digging proceeded until they found they were under the Houses of Parliament. Barrels of gunpowder were concealed under piles of logs . . ."

A fifteen-year-old writes this about night fears —

"Blackness in its darkest form
Creeps over all that dwell on earth,
And fills each separate being with a fear
Mysterious, overpowering and unfathomable.
The darkness hides away in deep oblivion
All things that daily give us confidence.
In daylight unperturbed we walk in leafy woods,
At night fear secretes itself in us.
Mundane things become silent ghosts,
Haunting our fearful minds.
Every shadow, every rustle, is a spectre hidden
In the depths of darkness.
Imagination plays his tricks and fear impedes our way.
But sleep locks out all thoughts of fear
And cheats him of his victims."

And the same pupil records this knowledge of the retina —

"The retina is a light sensitive coat which lines the inside of the eye behind the lens. It is made up of nerve cells and nerve fibres.

There are two kinds of nerve cells, rods and cones.

(a)   Rods — are stimulated by twilight.

(b)   Cones — are stimulated by daylight.

In some animals there are more of one sort than of the other, e.g., night animals such as owls have more rods than cones. Cones are thought to be responsible for colour vision. It is believed that they are stimulated by the three primary colours: red, green and blue.

The image formed on the retina is inverted and diminished. The fibres transmit impulses from the nerve cells to the brain. The nerve cells convert light stimuli into impulses. The fibres allow impulses to pass along them to the brain. All the fibres meet to form the optic nerve which ends in the brain."

A sixth-former wrote this about a journey —

"I sat alone
But a stranger was beside me.
We sat together,
Our bodies so close
That the heat transferred
And the pulsing arteries seemed in harmony.
So we were close together
And I was not alone.
But how could this be?
Our minds were separated by silence.
We were apart; far, far apart:
Alone in strange and different worlds.

It was odd the feeling of isolation
When all around
Cramming crowds
Stood, sat, talked;
So many of us
And our minds were apart,
Yet together.
We stood divided and united,
Made one in hostility to each other.

Are we one?
Am I alone?
Vibrating, noisy, air fills my mind,
Hot, blue smoke rises and overpowers."

And the same pupil recorded this following her scripture studies —

"John the Baptist preached repentance and the coming of God. He was not a prophet of doom; his job was to 'winnow the harvest' and 'separate the wheat from the chaff'; he told the people that they would not be saved just because they were Israelites but only because of their behaviour. He called men to be baptized as a sign that they repented of their sins and were willing to begin a new life.

Jesus went to be baptized by John; why did He do this? He had no sins, He was perfect and so had no need of repentance; perhaps it was because John's call was to the nation of Israel and as He was a member of the nation He felt He should go to be baptized.

He used the title 'Son of Man', which comes from the Book of Daniel; He looks upon this title as a symbol for Israel. True greatness is found in service and suffering. When He talks about the 'Son of Man' He is inviting the people of Israel to join Him in service and suffering. He did not claim to be the Messiah, but when asked point blank 'Are you the Messiah?' His answer was yes."

A Grammar school boy wrote the following two pieces — about a walk through the fog and the nitrogen cycle —

"The thick blanket smothered the dead city, silenced the void streets, threatened the lonely traveller, as I hobbled home one foot on, one foot off the pavement, kicking a rusty tin can into the mist before me. The minutes passed. I should be home soon sitting in front of a roaring log fire, and daring the choking smog to attack me there; but this was not our road or our house, was I lost? My feet were still savagely cleaving the fog, was I lost? Was I lost? My heart beat rapidly. I turned to run but a strange force compelled me onwards, ever onwards.

C

I was stopped by some invisible barrier, and then the magnetic sensation ceased. Of my own free will, I stumbled forward into a cobbled street quite deserted, but obviously inhabited yet with a stale, humid air. Directly in front of me stood a decrepit old shop with tiny green hammered glass windows and a frail wooden door with a greasy glass panel. Above the door was written one discernable word 'Antiques'."

"Nitrogen is found in quantity in the atmosphere, and, therefore, the nitrogen cycle starts with atmospheric nitrogen. This free gas is 'fixed' by nitrifying bacteria and lightning to form nitrates in the soil. In the lightning method, oxygen and nitrogen are combined by lightning during thunderstorms, producing nitric oxide and finally nitrogen peroxide. After this the nitrogen peroxide dissolves in rain to form a solution of nitric and nitrous acids, which are washed into the soil. The nitrates of the soil solution are then absorbed by plant roots to be used to form proteins and protoplasm of plants. This process is called protein synthesis. Atmospheric nitrogen is also 'fixed' by nodule bacteria on leguminous plants, and directly forms proteins and protoplasm in plants. Plants which are eaten by humans and animals help to make proteins and protoplasm in humans and animals."

Very many examples have been received from the schools showing that most children who use words well for one kind of writing will do so with equal facility for another.

The two main ways of using words — using them for factual statements or records and using them in poetry or to express feeling in prose — are both important to the educational process. The schools attach greater importance to the former than the latter, partly, no doubt, because it is thought to be easier to teach a child to make factual statements, partly because examinations demand them more often, and partly because the outside world expects this facility in every child. It is, however, open to question whether the ability to record easily is as valuable a stimulus to the child's personal development as the ability to express himself sensitively and powerfully, an ability which can give him great confidence and a deep satisfaction.

In most good Primary schools there is no distinction made between these two ways of writing. The curriculum shows few subject divisions, and the aim of much of the teaching is to expose a child to an experience which is within his understanding and will excite him to write or paint or model. The interest deriving from this experience will then in all likelihood be followed up by the reading of reference books and this in its turn will lead to further writing or drawing.

The experience may be a visit to a church or a canal, or it may derive from something new brought to the "nature corner" and may thus be associated with History, Geography or Nature Study. The important thing is that it will be the springboard for the child's writing which may take the form of a simple record or even of poetry; what he writes in this way is his English.

This is not so, however, in the Secondary schools, where the writing which results from experiences in the laboratories, or on an expedition, or in the craftroom, is not English but Science, or Biology, or Geography or Housecraft. In most of these schools English Language as such is something which is done during periods set apart for the purpose in the time-table. It used to be called English Grammar, it is now called English or even "English Language", and it looks as if it will very shortly be called "The Use of English".

One result of this dichotomy in the Secondary schools is that heads of departments and subject teachers seldom regard English as their concern, and the indifferent quality of the language used in their subjects becomes a handicap to the pupils at the next stage in their education and a source of vexation to the teachers who have to deal with them.

The written work in the next chapter has all been chosen to illustrate the pupils' personal writing.

Chapter III

CHILDREN'S WRITING

The work set out in this chapter is from two Infant schools, ten Junior schools, two Modern schools, and two Grammar schools. As has already been said, work has been chosen in the main from Junior schools, as it is with this age group that the greatest progress in this County has been made in recent years. It is important, however, to see how the work originates and what it can lead to, and therefore work by Infants and Secondary school pupils has been included in the collection. The teachers of all these children were asked to state briefly something of the principles and practice to which they hold. They were asked specifically to say what use they made of books of exercises and something of their teaching of spelling.

A teacher's statement in italics precedes the selection of work from each school, and views on the teaching of spelling are set out in Chapter IV.

WORK FROM TWO INFANT SCHOOLS

Work from a school, opened four years ago, which serves two housing estates in a South Yorkshire mining community. Most of children's fathers are miners and the daily routine of the home is based on the time of the father's "shift". A number of the mothers go out to work, mainly in sweet and clothing factories, as shop assistants or as domestic workers. Many of the children see few books at home other than comics or Christmas annuals.

The school has five classes; the headmistress has charge of a class and there are four full-time and one part-time assistant teachers. About twenty children are admitted each term; at present there are 183 children on roll. The younger children are grouped together, and the sixes and sevens are arranged in classes according to age.

The children at this school enjoy writing stories. Many of the stories they write are modelled on ones they know; for this reason alone they deserve good examples. The teachers attach much importance to the choice and presentation of stories and poetry in order to give the children worthwhile experiences. Stories are selected, not only for suitability for the age and interests of the group, but also for the quality of the language and the clarity of the plot. Often poetry is chosen to link up with some experience the children have had. They will ask again and again for a poem or a story that has appealed to them and, through this unconscious memorisation, words and phrases will become their own and will appear in their own writing.

The children are encouraged to make the experience and vocabulary of the stories they hear their own by writing them in their own words. The fact that the plot is known gives the security of a framework and leaves the children free to select the words they wish to use. At first, as in speech, fluency and good sense are all that matter, and nothing is allowed to hold back the children from expressing their thoughts. They are supplied with any words they need but are encouraged to be independent and to find words for themselves from any sources available. As fewer words have to be sought more thought is given to sequence of action. No work is rewritten and any corrections made are in the presence of the child concerned. Spelling is always related to the children's written work and, as with punctuation, most help is given individually as the need arises.

Once the children are interested in writing they are eager to practice their new skill and often write in the daily periods in which they may choose their own activities. It is during this free time that many imaginative stories are produced, but descriptions to supplement pictures, items of news, and records of excursions and experiments are written then too. A selection of suitable material is always available and work may be produced on paper, in booklets made by the children, or in large books made by the teacher. Unlined paper and thick pencils are used throughout the school.

It is not sufficient for the children to have something to write about, and suitable materials and opportunities to write: as a speaker requires a listener, a writer needs a reader. The teachers in this school, by showing a real interest in what the children have to say, do much to encourage them and the children thrive in their company.

Boy age 6.

Our Jane

Our Jane is two.
She plays with a boy and
she has white hair and
she has blue eyes and
she has a runny nose and
she can't talk and
she eats biscuits and
she's fat and
she pinched my biscuits and
she's got a bike like an old cronk and
she plays with my train and
she's a monkey when telly's on.
She plays about.
She plays up and down.
They let her.

Boy age 7.

Cave Men

Once upon a time there was two cave men with brims on their hats, and they went to a little stream to get fish, and one day a typhoon came and the two cave men had to take everything into the cave so it would not get blown away, and they had to live in the cave for ninety-nine years. And when they came out it was sunshining, and they went to the stream to get a drink and some fish, and they caught twenty apiece, and they had forty altogether. And in the light time they would have a swim, and then they would fish for tea, and then they would lie down and go to sleep and dream, and their dreams came true.

Boy age 6.

The Christmas Story

Early next morning they got up and Joseph tucked in his long coat, and Mary tucked up her long cloak, and she wrapped up the baby's clothes, and Mary jumped up on the donkey's back, and the donkey's hoofs clattered on the stone cobbles, and they reached the hillside. What a good ride it is, said Joseph, and Mary said, What a good ride it is. So did Joseph. He thought it was, and it was a good ride. Joseph had his staff to help him to walk right because it was a long, long journey to Bethlehem so he had his staff to make him go big strides. They journeyed all day long, and when evening came it was nearly dark, and Joseph lighted a fire, and Mary got some food out of a plastic bag, and they slept with their long cloaks round themselves.

Girl age 7 (a slow learner).

The Baby Bird

Once upon a time there was a little baby bird and he was a little rascal in the nest. He fell down down down flat on his bum, and he went looking for his mother, and he cried and cried till his mother came.

Girl age 6.

God sent Mary home, and a beautiful Spring morning came, a big lovely Spring morning came, and Jesus grew up to be a strong, big boy, and Jesus was happy and happy and happy. He said to his friends, You are beautiful and beautiful and beautiful, and I do love you so much, and I will be your friend for years and years and years, till you are a teddy boy. You are 7 years old now. You are a big boy, and you will be 8 if you be quick.

Girl age 7.

Extract from *The Story of Romulus and Remus*.

The River Tiber rocked Romulus and Remus fast asleep, and in a while Romulus woke up and started to cry because he was hungry, and he woke Remus up and Remus started to cry because he was hungry, and the River Tiber thought they must want some milk, so he thought when he saw some mud he would make the children go on the bank. And on the bank there was a hill, and and on the hill there was a cave, and in the cave there was a mother wolf who had five very young children, and they had just been born and had their supper, and they were biting and scratching, And the wolf thought, I am thirsty, so she set off to the river, and when she heard a funny noise she pricked up her ear, and she went a bit farther and pricked up both ears, and she did wonder.

The wolf crept carefully on to the River Tiber, and the noise got louder and nearer, and when she got up she saw the twin babies crying. She gave them some milk and they started to gurgle, and they gurgled a vry lot indeed. Then the Mother wolf picked up Romulus by the scruff of the neck and took him to the cave and said, Do not harm the babies. Then she did the same with Remus, took him by the scruff of his neck and troted back to the cave. And then she put them on the floor, and every time they cried she gave them some milk, and every time they got sleepy she cuddled them.

Boy age 6.

Tulips

I have painted some tulips. I have painted them red, yellow, black, a tiny bit of white and a green stalk, and a white pistil, and yellow stamens, yellow and red petals, and black pollen. And there is a tiny bit of red on the end of each petal, and there is purple inside of the pollen, and at the bottom of the stalk it looks like bubbles, and it feels like some satin, and it looks like a rainbow, and the petals look like hearts.

Boy age 7.

Billy Smart's Caravan

When the circus came to Potefract I went to see the circus. It was a lot of fun. After the circus we went and looked at some of the caravans. We came across Billy's caravan. We did not notice a robber hiding in the grass. When we had gone, the robber got out of his hiding place. He stole the caravan. Me and my dad saw the caravan taking off. We leaped for the caravan. We got on to the top of the caravan. I nearly fell off the roof. I caught hold of the rim of the caravan. My dad lifted (me) on to the top. We saw a porthole was open. There was just enough room for me to get through. I walked along until I got to the door. My dad clambered along the top. I opened the door and in came my dad. He hit the robber on his head with the butt of the rifle. My dad took over the wheel. When we got back to the circus Billy rewarded us with three pounds each. The robber got sent to jail.

Work from an Infants' school of 80–90 children.

We are housed in a building nearly a hundred years old and typical of hundreds more of that age. We share this building with the Junior school. On one side we look out on to a busy and noisy main road, on another our view is blocked by the toilets and on a third we have waste land and pit stacks. This doesn't worry us particularly, as by the time the term is a week old there are usually so many things, animate and inanimate, to be investigated inside and outside the classroom, so many things to be done that the only pinch we feel is lack of space. We have no hall — just a small room called by the children "the Singing Room" (which is also the Head Teacher's room, stock room, etc.) into which the children migrate when they feel the need for more space.

The children are a cross section of those found in most of our Primary schools. They come from working-class homes, most of them good, some not so good. There is no streaming. Each child is helped and encouraged to develop at his or her own pace. There is very little class teaching.

We are fortunate in having a piece of waste land near the school where a pond has formed through subsidence. The children take a very lively interest in what is found there, both in and out of school time, and this is the core of our work.

We are an active lively community — busy all day long finding out some-thing — that the newt is casting its skin, that the pond looks thousands of miles deep when it is still and that the waves break up the reflections, that pottery mould is better than soap to carve, and that "this book says just what you told us about our caterpillars eating".

In our school, the environment — home, classroom, school and the outdoors — is the hub and basis of all our work. We find that, having made the environment their own through seeing, hearing, touching, etc., the children, secure in their experiences, write with eagerness, spontaneity and fluency. The vocabulary is authentically enriched and one experience illuminates and explains another. Furthermore, the children develop an enquiring mind and through their own initiative go much further than we would have thought of taking them.

Boy age 5.

> Today it was raining like Billeo. I couldn't breathe with the wind. It turned me round and round. If I look forward I will get wet and I will catch a cold I could not Breathe. It was horrid my socks were wet through as well.

Boy age 6.

> We have got some tulips They are yellow we have got a red one coming out. when they are fully out they are like a cake stand with a handle at the top. Our red one is not fully out yet our red one will be a beautiful one it has a bit of orangey yellow mixt in it. It is like a bonfire with the red in the middle and the yellow round the side like flames shooting up in the air when they are ready to come fully out there petals open slowly and then they are fully out.

Boy age 6.

The New Nest

> When we went for our walk yesterday we found that the swans had finished their nest But two weeks ago it was raggy shaggy and ugly we wondered how ever she could lay her eggs in it. But when we went yesterday afternoon it was a beautiful nest like an eagles nest. the Miss Swan was asleep and the father swan was guarding the fort and if any enemies came he would stretch out his long neck and peck them with his beak.

Girl age 6.

Long long ago there lived a live leaf. But one day some water came and then mud then water then mud. Then at last it stopped and the leaf was changed and it was a stone leaf. It was a grey stone with the leaf in it. My dad found out in the pit. He brought it home. Then I brought it to school. Some have animals and some have a leaf all rocks are made in earth some are little and some are not. We have got a fossil Miss B . . . brought it some rooks are shot up from a volcanoes.

Girl age 6.

This morning Denise has brought some lovely catkins to school She has brought some hazel catkins and some willow catkins the willow catkins are like a little silver mitten with a little black bud the hazel catkins are honey coloured they are long and hanging they are like lambs tails they are very nice they are in a shady brown bowl they remind me of spring.

Boy age 7.

The Poor Swan

At Christmas it was very very cold colder than it has been for nearly a hundred years and all the ponds were frozen over Dunneys pond was frozen over too. so me and Geoffrey decided to go and skate on the pond. When we got there we saw a Big white thing near the nest so we all skated over and we saw it was one of our swans So I sat on the nest with it and I put my coat over it We thought it was dead and it was dead real. So the others went home to get some tools to get the swan out of the cold ice so we got it out with the axe and an hammer and some shovels and a pick and then we took the swan carefully out of the ice put it in a warm cover and took it to our secret cave.

Boy age 7.

When we went on our walk a couple of days ago. We found some pots made of chalk and there name is pottery moulds. They are used to make cups and jugs. And basins and other kinds of china. When we got back to school we broke them in two and made all kinds of models. We carved them with a knife we pretended to be sculptors. There was a famous sculptor. His name was Henry Moore. He lived at Castleford and went to Grammar School. He has carved many statues like statues outside a palace. Nearly everybody in the world knows him. He has flitted now.

Boy age 7.

The Adventures of our Cabbage White Caterpillars

How lucky our cabbage white caterpillars are all through this terrible weather. They have fastened themselves to the side of the tank and made a pale green chrysalis and stayed there until the warm weather comes again and then we will see butterflies in the class room and the holes in the top of chrysalises. our hawk will come out a small pink Moth the Elephant hawk makes a rusty coloured brown chrysalis and it is like a bullet with spot and markings on the sides of it there will be golden butterflies and white ones coming on the dandelions and the bees and wasps will be gathering nectar from the dandelions and will Make honey. The grass will grow again. the buds will be leaves and the sun will shine again and make the plants grow and the flowers will open and there will be more cygnets on the pond and the birds singing again.

WORK FROM TEN JUNIOR SCHOOLS

Work from an unstreamed Junior Mixed and Infant school of 430 pupils serving a National Coal Board housing estate. The fathers of all but one of the children whose work is quoted are miners; the exception is a railway worker. The school has been open four years. During its erection hundreds of pounds worth of wilful damage was done to the building. Since it was opened no damage has been done either to the building or the flowers and shrubs which surround it, apart from one window being deliberately broken by a child whose parents refused on religious grounds to allow him to attend it. Since it was opened the Probation Officer reports an improvement in behaviour which is "beyond belief".

Just as we learn to talk by talking, we learn to write by writing. We do not learn to write by filling in blanks or by writing English exercises. For children there must be a reason for writing; they must become eager and excited enough to want to write; they soon appreciate that in writing you have put your thoughts down permanently in front of you, whereas the spoken word is lost. We must consider how children learn, and how we can create the urge for them to express themselves in writing.

Children learn mostly from that which is around them, and from the use of their senses. These impressions so gained will depend a great deal on interests which will vary considerably. If children are interested they listen more carefully, look more closely, and touch more sensitively. With interest there is created the element of wonder, the most precious element of life. We appreciate that with the acquisition of interest and wonder at the things around us we have the basis for the expressing of ideas in the written and spoken word. We must continually aim at giving the children experiences through which they will develop. They may be from geography, history, nature study or some other subject, but it is all part of the school's "English". We must think less in terms of the subjects a child must learn and more in terms of experiences they can enjoy and gain interest from. Where can children look for sources of inspiration? To a large extent this depends on the classroom environment and on the teacher's subtlety in using his own imagination and inventiveness to put experience in their way, since it must be recognised that all schools are not situated in a pleasant environment.

We find that there arise two distinct patterns of written English being used right through the school.

1. The first is the English which comes from direct observation. This is the straightforward writing or recording of statements of fact, a stimulated looking as through the eyes of another person. It could be from reading a book, hearing a story, watching television or from poetry and literature. Historical, geographical and scientific accounts are examples of this particular pattern of expression.

In this type of writing form and shape, e.g. spelling, handwriting, punctuation, can be brought to the children's notice. We must remember however to be careful not to overstress techniques and form to the extent of destroying confidence. They are important however and all work done by children must be seen, preferably in their presence. Common mistakes should be marked depending on the ability of the child to understand the correction.

2. The other pattern we find being used by the children is the expressive English based on sensory experiences. This pattern is completely different from the English of recorded fact as it is a personal response where the outer world is shut out and the child has the psychological satisfaction of expressing his own personal feelings without the restrictive fear of marking and correction. In this type of expression we are more concerned with what is said than how it is said. This is writing at a conscious level from direct experiences. We mostly go out of the classroom to gain these experiences but many opportunities can be created in the classroom itself. Nature provides us with many suitable experiences such as the wind, mist, rain, snow, etc. Visits to local places of interest can often stimulate this type of expressive writing.

One other type of written expression is of course imaginative writing. In writing imaginatively the children are drawing unconsciously from the two types of experiences mentioned above.

We must be mindful in our encouragement to children to write and in putting a value on fluency that we do not imply that there is virtue in sheer length of writing unrelated to what has to be said. Similarly the compiling of a diary or topic book, when interest in it is dead, can only provide a monotonous and dull response.

In conclusion, may I restate that to the children there must be something to write about and a reason for writing. They must be given frequent opportunities to write, they require time to finish and they must not be over anxious about accuracy or lacking in respect for the reader. Furthermore, there is in my mind no doubt that the readiness of children to write and the quality of their writing is influenced by opportunities to express their thoughts through other materials such as paint, clay, fabric and dramatic movement.

Girl age 11.

Market Day

Rushing, talking loudly, and arguing, the busy Saturday shoppers trudge determinedly to the stalls. Colourful clothes are being worn by these people on this dull December day. Men with their goods, step out onto the wet pavement to try to persuade the busy people to take heed and offer to buy goods. Doors of shops are creaking and banging, while women and children come onto the pavements with their shopping baskets nearly full. Green, blue and red buses, lorries, and other vehicles rumble along the bumpy uneven road. People, small, tall and thin dash about, near the road side. Groceries and other colourful goods are seen, piled high on the low, wooden stalls. Buildings, tall, strong and straight, stand upright in the many streets of Castleford. Life, noise, and movement is seen in this rush for the sales, as sturdy men trudge reluctantly to the vast shops and stalls. Apples, oranges and grapefruits are seen on this busy market day. All these goods are gathered together to see what will be left on this busy market day.

Boy age 11.

The Dodgems

Sparks shot from the long pole as it scraped across the network of wire. Cars of all colours were driven into each other. Bangs and crashes rang out over the blaring music. Green and red lights flashed on and off, and added to the excitement as people laughed and charged at each other in their compact cars. Floorboards rattled, as one after another the cars trundled around and in and out of each other. Everyone keeps a wary eye open, for an attacker from behind. The steering wheel is frantically turned around as people try to avoid collisions. You look around, the gay colours, and the fast movement, hold you awestricken. All the fun of the Fair is around you. You feel happy, excited and gay. A volley of shots rang out at the rifle range, and small tin figures fall.

You never want to leave this colourful place full of splendour and joy. Round and round you go, trying to dodge charges made by people enjoying the fun of the Fair. In return you try to ram the cars of other people and if you miss you swerve, trying to avoid hitting the rail. Eventually the cars drew to, and I was quick to rush onto other rides and stalls.

Girl age 11.

Gipsy Life

I walked along the beautiful country lane, when a brightly coloured caravan caught my eye. I walked on until I came upon an encampment of the loveliest caravans I ever saw. Blues, reds, yellows and greens of all shades and sizes were there to met my eye. Among all this: merry gipsies walked women made pegs and baskets while the men worked to get money to buy things needed to keep a family. The children went with small, thin, shoes on their feet. These poor children suffered greatly. Pots and pans were scattered upon the hard, brown ground. All the people of this camp made pegs or flowers. They all wore things given to them. Children wondered through the familiar forests of caravans and wagons. The only live stock he has are hens, dogs, and horses. The hens have beautiful feathers of oranges and browns. Looking at them I could see how plump they were. The gipsies seemed to look after these hens. The dogs were thin and shaggy compared to the hens, while the horses were dirty and unattended.

I went closer to the caravans and the smell of logs burning met my nose. I could also smell food cooking in the open air. Although all the adventure tempted me I don't think I would be able to stand all the suffering and hardships these people endured. Everything about the gipsy camp seemed enchanting. Especially the gaily painted caravans and the friendly gipsy folk. After an exciting time among the gipsies I ran back home with caravans drifting through my mind.

Girl age 10.

A Squirrel

A soft bushy tail brings beauty to this nut brown animal. Small beady eyes flash in the sunlight as it looks mysteriously around. Small feathery hairs curve to a point. As it sits up, he proudly displays his small white shirt. Delicate ears travel to a point as a proud head rises. A small nose juts out to the air around him. Long black whiskers never once twitch as there it stands so lonely. A small pathetic face goes straight to your heart. A small bony finger ends with a terrifying claw as it clasps to another hand. Rough looking feet dig into the ground as it keeps a steady balance. Strong looking teeth forever want to bite a strong looking acorn. A long slender nut brown arm looks delicate but not harmless. But as it sits in dismal surroundings it never will see that homely wood again.

Boy age 11.

A Stoat

Needle-like fangs are enclosed in a snarling vicious mouth. This ferocious enemy is unwanted by many a hen, rabbit, and mouse. Ready to pounce on an unwary animal offering a challenge to all his foes. Only swiftness and bite, lie between him and starvation. His back is arched in fury. Fore legs are stiff, hind legs bent and ready to pounce, tail low and curved. Tinted brown and grey, not at all like his pure white winter coat. His black shiny eyes glint evilly. Grey whiskers streak backwards like his stroked fur. Brown, tan, fawn, and nut brown are also the colours in his summer coat. How delicate and innocent, the teeth may seem, but once they sank into the flesh of a frightened animal. The tiny paws once carried a living Stoat over the countryside.

D

Boy age 11.

An Interesting Character

Nearly every Sunday he takes Mass, and as he holds his pale hands together they shake as if he is nervous. Everyone seems to enjoy Mass more when the Father takes it, his hands freely move about as he talks to you. A shy handsome face attracts most of the girls at any dances held at the school. A timid voice seems to understand our troubles, and it seems so warm and loving. Slowly he walks into the playground talking to children about their work and play. At our sports he will watch and show a broad happy smile, gladly he will show you how to play. Everyone, young and old, always gather round him to hear him preach or to hear him say a prayer. His home is under the ancient chapel with an old lady as his maid, who cleans the little flat while he works. Many a pretty girl wishes he was not a man who gives up his life for God. Never have I seen such a priest who is kind, warm and gentle to all, no matter how much we have sinned.

Boy age 10.

Boiler Room

Three large boilers stand in a gigantic room, nestled beside machinery of all kinds and sizes. Like a red hot furnace, it sends heat drifting through every crevice and cranny. Dusty walls can be seen towering over small machines which seem to never stop. It feels like sitting round a camp fire at full blaze, and then a slight draught cools everything. Thick dust covers all, giving a feeling of mystery and dampness. Long red pipes are positioned along every place where an accident may occur, as they spray water on machines if they might catch on fire. Large pillars hold the room up and support the gigantic machines. Like a boisterous party, the machines roar on and on, camouflaging all by their terrific din. As my unsteady body trudges on, the heat becomes even hotter and hotter until the opening of a window refreshes us all. As we leave this miraculous wonder, thoughts of the future entered my head.

Boy age 11.

Control Room

Cold steel steps lead to the control room of an enormous power station. Warm air blows to my body as huge machines roar. Every second of the day loud buzzing is heard from the spinning turbines. As the door closes all the buzzing noises disappear. Long grey panels seem to be decorated with switches and knobs. Handles and lights are turned on to make the machines work. Men in white overalls walk about testing the temperature of the roaring machines. I felt frightened while looking through the metal floor. Clocks and dials indicate whether a certain machine is working. Each knob is very important to make electricity. Every man who works in the control room has to be skilled. Sparks can be seen as a worker mends one of the machines. Machines of all shapes and sizes are seen from the the windows of the compact control room. Each of these men in this control room are responsible for all the electricity in our houses of today.

Boy age 11.

The Furnace

A maze of rusted pipes twist, coil and bend around an enormous room. A complicated mass of deafening machinery working night and day to produce electricity. The odour of oil comes from a substance dripping from a network of pipes. Thick coal dust carpets a section of concrete floor. Great iron walls hold in the licking flames of the large oil furnace. I slip on the pair of thick green glassed goggles over my eyes. The small steel door in the furnace wall opens and I look into the roasting flames. They blindingly dance up and down like bolts of lightening. My eyes almost burn amid the heat and flames of the furious inferno. Like something insane it seems to eat away at the air. It fights and swirls and attacks at imagined foes. It jeers and laughs, shouting defiance at anyone trying to brave the flames and enter its domain. It tries to push and expand, but the small door shuts and the flames are imprisoned once again.

Boy age 11.

Inside the Cooling Tower

There I stood, at the foot of a small door just about to enter. I paused for a moment, then I went in. Great puffs of dirty steam filled the tower. I walked along a path, it had slime all over it. The slime looked like whirlpools. There was nothing to be heard, only the sound of water as it ran through the pleats of iron girders. I felt as if I was a mouse trapped in a cage. I came to some steps, they were black and dirty. Looking upwards, I see how tall the tower really is. It stands bold and straight like a church steeple. At first you feel dizzy, then sick, but after a while it wears off. Now and then I feel sick, but not all the time. Sometimes a spray of water splashes the side of the path. Everywhere is cold and damp, it feels like rain or drizzle. On the pipes are little air bubbles all over them. I turn to go but think what a wonderful experience I have had today. Leaving the tower, I feel the fresh air swirl into my lungs.

A small school built 65 years ago and housing about 100 boys and girls of 7 to 11. The mining community which the school serves is a drab and uninviting village adjoining a small industrial town.

This work is the result of experiences which the children have had, either at school or in their home background. These expressions are their own. The vocabulary or "expressions" have not been given or suggested. Vocabulary and "expressions" are given to the children in readings from literature. Such literature has not been chosen to provide vocabulary for any particular experience but to provide a background of vocabulary from which the child can select for his own purpose. Grammatical constructions are learned from this context of reading and not by "exercises" from exercise books. True practice in the correct use of grammatical constructions is provided by the pupils use of them in their own work. This ensures that what they do is at their own level and has a real meaning.

Every child is taught phonetic spelling and word-building but again rules and exceptions in spelling are learned from their reading and their desire to spell correctly in their own work. There are no exercises in learning to spell words not associated with their experience.

This I feel ensures that the "form" of their writing is at their own level and is such as to ensure that the children can express the "content" of their writing without being hampered by techniques beyond their ability.

Girl age 10.

Our Back Street

From the old blackening shop hung a torn, dirty advertisement, limp and wet after a shower of rain. Mingled shouts from children playing ball come echoing down the street as they play round the old gas-lamp. Two women were standing at the gate of their neighbour bragging about their new coat or pair of shoes or talking about their families or the doings of their neighbours. Most of the children usually crowded round the old lampost at the end of the street playing or talking about television. It is a dirty but merry street and no proper road only coke and dirt. Black soot is caked to the bricks and wispy smoke comes from the square chimney pots. The grumpy old men wearily sit down in the scraggy gardens talking of their younger days. The dustbins were in an awful condition but nobody cared. The street was never empty.

Boy age 10.

Morning in the Allotments

As we went out of the school I felt a light fresh breeze. The grass was damp with dew like millions of tiny pieces of glass sparkling and glittering in the sunlight. The sun was a yellowish golden light spreading all over. It was still a little misty but it was only a hazy mist and I felt fresh and clean and fit. The black brattish on the huts was white with frost. When I walked past the pig-stys I saw a woman taking pig swill into the pigs. They were grunting and squealing loudly and greedily. Some pigeons were flying in the cool air tippling and twisting in flight. They were circling and sometimes they turned and went around the other way. They fly very fast and flap their wings very fast. Some ducks in a garden were busy eating and drinking. Their beaks clack together when they eat. Their beaks were yellow but muddy with sticking them in the mud. They were dirty and when they drank they put up their backs and they waddled as they walked. Every so often they wag their tails in a humorous manner.

Girl age 10.

Cobwebs on a Foggy Day
Wispy cobwebs strung the fences,
Loosely drooping everywhere,
Like pearl beads.
They fade away if you touch them.
They hide in every crack;
They veil the trees
And carpet the grass.
Cold and grey
They blanket the world,
Patching up holes.

Girl age 10.

Our Street at Night
The lamps glisten with the raindrops. It is all silent except for footsteps on the pavement. I can see the pond shining through the houses. I hear the voice of Mrs. E . . . shouting Colin and Paul in for bed. Her voice is loud and shrill and it echoes through the darkness. The cars flash their lights as they drive up the street and they make shadows on the fence. When my father's on nights I stand and watch him disappear into the darkness.

Girl age 10.

The Fog

Damp enveloping fog
Rising up to the invisible sky.
Clinging, heavy fog
Spreading its blankets on the trees.
A tiny hollow becomes
A mystic bottomless hole.
It has hung the grass
With crystal dewy beads
No longer graceful are the swans
All their beauty gone.
Damp and cold they are,
Their Stately feathers ruffled.

Girl age 10.

At the Baths

I will always remember the first time I went to the baths. As I entered through the doors I could hear distant hollow noises coming from the baths. It gave me a queer feeling inside me. The hollow noises seemed to echo, muffled and dull, over the bath. In the locker room the noise was muffled and distant. In the water the noise was louder than ever. The harsh, crisp sound of someone jumping in shattered the echoing noise. Then the shrill clear sound of the whistle broke the noise and everyone hurried off chattering quietly. The noise seemed to be trapped inside the baths and couldn't get out. It seemed to bounce off the water up to the ceiling and then bounce back to the water again.

Boy age 10.

Sound

Sound is everywhere on the earth. It is in the air, it is on the ground. Yesterday we went to Dunny's pond. We could hear the crisp, crunchy sound of gravel under our feet. We could hear the cock crowing, a loud noise, a clear sound, a bright sound. The wind in our ears was like a blanket being shaken or the distant sound of thunder, muffling all other sounds. The sound of feet on dry grass, a whispering kind of sound; a train shunting up and down the track, a powerful sound, a softish sound; the clanging of wagons joining on to each other, the brakes screeching and scraping, an annoying sound; the birds chirping, a short, clean, sharp sound.

Boy age 10.

An Hour by a Rough Sea

I can remember that hour I walked on the sands by a very rough sea. The waves crashed down so hard I could feel the trembling of them on me. It sounded like bricks tumbling down from an old house when it is being knocked down. While the waves were thundering down seagulls sounded as though they were screaming and crying in the blustering wind. The wind sounded like somebody who can't whistle trying to. The waves when they had crashed down slithered like worms over the rocks and pebbles.

Boy age 10.

"David"

He is nine years old and lives at Normanton. He is a rough kind of boy with his pullover ruffled up, his shirt hanging half in and half out. He has a tangled mass of hair in knots very untidy. He speaks in a rough mumbling voice with a bit of Yorkshire in it. He has a pair of uncleaned shabby shoes with laces half undone. But on Sundays when he goes to church he is polite and generous and will share things with you, and he goes with a nice pair of shining shoes and clean hands and face and with a quif in his hair with a neat parting. When he walks he walks slowly and then he will walk a bit faster. He sniffs a lot because he can't find his handkerchief.

Girl age 10.

The Wind

The wind roared by us like the thunder
And the smoke blew everywhere
And the gulls high in the sky
Screamed as they went by.
The ripples in the water went running
And the reeds were all dead
And there were no fish about
Because the wind had come today.
The water came running by
And all because of the Westerly wind
And all because of the Westerly wind
And our hair blew all over
But us children do not bother.

Girl age 10.

Autumn by the Pond

The pond was still and quiet. Only a few ripples were on it. The two swans and three cygnets stood on their island preening themselves. After they had satisfied themselves they slowly slid into the water. First went the parents then the young ones, all in a row like soldiers. The young swans' feathers were fluffy the old one's smooth and white. They swam to the edge of the pond smoothly. The older ones stayed still. The reflections of the things round the pond were solid. They were so solid that you could see the smoke from a house. The rushes were all greens and browns and all bent the same way.

Work from a school of 120 Junior girls from working class homes. They live either in houses built 50 years or more ago in long drab rows or in the houses of a new housing estate. They are on the whole well cared for.

Our first task is to build up a teacher–child relationship of confidence and trust. This allows the child to converse and write freely at all times, knowing that she will never be rejected, and her ideas will always be sympathetically received. Indeed, she becomes eager to share her thoughts and experiences with her teacher. But there can be no expression without impression so we develop the senses and try to increase the children's awareness of their environment. By enriching their personal experiences we hope the knowledge so gained will be stored away and perhaps used at a later date.

Throughout the school the children read extensively and selected stories and poems are read to them. Descriptive passages are used to teach any special aspect of English, and from an early age the girls use dictionaries. In the third and fourth years every child has a dictionary besides building up a personal vocabulary book. Indeed, the girls become so familiar with dictionaries that these books have now become exciting storehouses of words rather than books containing dull, monotonous lists of words. In this way spelling is learned naturally by the children and from the reading punctuation becomes increasingly familiar.

Incidental teaching is given individually when the teacher is marking a child's work and often alternative words may be suggested for future reference.

We believe that children can learn much more effectively by these methods than by working out a series of exercises from an English exercise book.

Girl age 9.

An Old Man I Know

I know an old man who is very fond of walking and when he walks he seems to rock from side to side like a baby's cradle when somebody is rocking it. One of his eyes has no black pupil in it so he is blind in that eye. His skin is crinkled and wrinkled like a piece of crepe paper. He has a pipe somewhere but he never smokes it. He always smokes Woodbine cigarettes. He seems to get tired easily and is forever sitting down for a rest when he is doing something. He used to be able to play the piano but now his fingers have grown too old and stiff it makes it quite difficult for him. He has false teeth and has a habit of taking them out and running his tongue over his gums and then putting his teeth back again. One thing I've noticed though. He never takes his top set out, always his bottom set. He has lived by himself since his wife died over three years ago but he seems quite happy and still has a lot of fun left in him even after all these years.

Girl age 10.

An Old Lady I Know

This old lady used to be the bank cleaner and we got very friendly with her. Her real name is Mrs. W . . . but we call her Weddy. She is ninety-two just after Christmas, but even though she's very old she still can have a bit of fun and she's very rarely sad.

Weddy's fingers have grown so much that she has no nails because her fingers have over-lapped them.

Her face is wizened and wrinkled and she's nearly deaf, her mouth is a round shape like an O and when she's finished speaking her mouth seems to twitch.

She can not walk properly and she hobbles and she's never without an old umbrella which she walks with.

Her hair is dark grey and she wears it in a bun on the back of her head.

She lives by herself in a little cottage in S . . . Lane.

One day Weddy came to our house to visit us and all the time she was there she kept her hat on even though she took her coat off. She wears very long clothes mostly black. When she went from our house she had to go down the stairs and it nearly took her all day because she went down one at a time and my daddy had to hold her arm and take her down and then she was slow. (There are 42 steps)

Weddy is a very nice person and very friendly, and I shall be very sad when she dies.

Girl age 11.

A Foggy Day

Last Friday was a very foggy day. It played havoc with the motorists and car drivers, especially in built up places. The light barely flickered through the clammy mist, even the light that did penetrate was only very dim, everything seemed icy-cold, damp and ghostly. People walked cautiously peering ahead, because the light from the head-lamps of the vehicles just managed to filter through the dense mass of wet, greasy, misty atmosphere. Castleford was almost deserted outside. Flower's grass and trees were moist with the water vapour, that had condensed on them. It seemed to be like an opaqeu veil covering the land as far as you could see, almost like a grey coverlet too. By the time it was dark it was very black and you could not tell in which direction you were going, hardly anything was visible. At any moment you might see a faint flicker telling you there was a car coming round the corner. The honks of the motor-car horns seemed muffled and eerie.

Girl age 9.

Market Day

On open market day there is a hurrying and scurrying a hustle and bustle a gossiping nineteen to the dozen you can hear babies screaming their heads of while their mothers chatter and shout. I hope you don't go home with a headache like I do. People are rumageing to find good bargains you see people dashing, pushing, shoving. If you try to get to one stall you end up at another. Sometimes people will gossip all morning. You go from one stall to another and come back and there they are still chattering.

Girl age 9.

Sounds of the Night

When I go to bed I feel drowsy. I drag my heavy feet up the stairs. My nightie trails behind me. I hold my doll by her arm, my case of dolls clothes weighs my arm down because it is so heavy but at last I reach the top. I drag myself into my bedroom and flop onto the bed like a rag doll. After a few minutes my daddy turns off the light on the stairs. As I lie in bed I listened I could hear the soft ticking whisper of the clock. I could hear the mens muffled voces on T.V., the gentle moter of the cars as they stop and the roar of the engine as they start up again, and the gentle murmer of the dog as she lay dreaming by the fire, It is all quiet then suddenly my doll falls out of bed with a thud.

Girl age 11.

The New Shoes

We set out, Mummy and I, we were going into the town. I was delighted for I was to have a pair of new shoes, they were to be for school. When we got to the town we went in a shoe shop. I saw a few pairs of shoes but I didn't like any of them, the woman then brought out another pair of shoes brown and ugly. Mummy liked them, I looked at her in horror unable to speak surely, surely she wouldn't buy them. But the purchase was complete she had bought them, I pinched myself to make sure it wasn't a dream, unluckily for me it wasn't.

For a moment I was surprised and starteled that she could buy such things, then when that feeling had left me it was replaced by anger. I was furious but I didn't say anything until I got home then I told Mummy that I would never wear the horrid shoes and went upstairs in a temper. The next day I was sorry for what I had said and I apologised to my mother, but I was still dismayed and disappointed, and I never liked those shoes. I wore them out as fast as I could.

Girl age 9.

In the Firelight

As I sit in front of the fire I can see a tiny spark in the flames as they dance and dart about. I suddenly feel drowsy and my limbs feel heavy. My eyes get blurred and I get hotter I feel dizzy and my head rolls round in circles as my eyes follow the flames where ever they go Then I cannot stand it any longer and I move back to get cool but I still follow the flames untill my head droops to my knees and I fall asleep.

Girl age 9.

Noises of the Night

I went to bed last night feeling miserable because I could not watch Harpers West One. I dragged myself up the stairs and bounced heavily into bed. I said my prayers and kissed my mummy goodnight. Then I lay awake listening to the noises of the night. I heard the running of high-heeled shoes vibrating on the stone paving. Then I heard the roaring start of a motor bike I hear drunken singing. I hear people banging on doors. I heard two dogs yelping. Then I heard the beginning of Maigret.

From the junior class of a two-teacher Junior Mixed and Infants school. There are 28 children in the class varying in age between 7 and 11. The school is one of several serving a small but highly industrial community.

In order that the children may write sincerely they are given as often as possible the opportunity of listening to, touching, seeing and smelling interesting things around them both in and out of school. This feeding of the senses with first-hand experience calls forth differing responses from individual children and it is necessary that these responses be expressed through such media as language, clay, paint, fabric, movement or sound.

In expressing a response through language many children need help from the teacher. By discussion and questioning the teacher helps each child to clarify his response in terms of language and often a child needs to unearth little-used words from a past experience in order to come really close to what he wishes to say.

The children hear a story or poetry daily, so that their language experience is a rich one. Opportunity is also given daily for each child to write on any subject he chooses and this "free-writing" complements and utilises the work done by the class as a result of direct observation. No books of English exercises are used as I feel they call for prescribed responses and often limit language experience rather than extend it.

Boy age 7.

The Trees
In the wood the leaves are dark,
But not in the park.
In the park the leaves are light,
What a beautiful sight!

Boy age 7.

A Remain

On Wednesday a fire came,
    A big fire.
On Wednesday a fire came,
    A jig fire.
It came and went and saw
    and spent
The value of the building.

But now it is a ghost
Because it took the most.
It was a century old
But now it is very cold.
It will never work again
And so it is a remain.

Boy age 7.

No Good

There's nothing that remains,
The house was all in flames,
The rags are all scorched
And nobody thought
What to do with the remains.
Nobody did any thinking,
What to do with the building.
Isn't it a shame.

Boy age 10.

A Giant's Voice

The organ is the king of instruments. It can make a loud, broad, triumphant sound. The great organ booms as the organist presses the keys with great skill. It is a noise that could drive an army on to battle. The foot keys creep and haunt the place. It rumbles as the wind vibrates against the great pipes. It is a grand instrument. It is like a giant as it thunders its voice and the very timid sounds it makes are so gentle and calm.

Boy age 10.

Misty Morning

As we were walking we heard the noises of one or two lonely birds. In the fields there was a ground mist which was about two feet high. In the distance is a buzzing crane working at the draining for the railways and there were the trains which clanged to a standstill. Then with a shrill note the whistle makes a deafening noise and the steam comes pouring out into a grey, dirty smoke. Then a four-bell-call is sent for a parcels train or empty coaching stock for Mirfield.

It was fairly cold but the houses were like grey ghosts in the far distance. Back at school we could see a bird which was all fluffed up.

Boy age 11.

The Fire

As I looked at the old mill I wondered what it would be like if I were that mill, sitting in solitude without sympathy. How lonely that old, burnt-out mill must be, wrapped in deathly silence with the crumbled mass of stone and wood and twisted and slashed metalwork.

As you look the cold, fevery sound of creaking timber is shattering the horrible silence which covers the loud noise of the cars and lorries passing in the distance. Oh how I hate to see the dead skeleton of a ghostly place hoping for renewal.

As you look at it you wish you were far, far away. The straggling girders are now lying around like meat of a dead animal after being attacked by a lit-up enemy. As you look at it, it looks like a whole lot of rocking horses. Then you see charred wood strewn all around.

The deathly silence is suddenly torpedoed by chirping and twittering birds which are still wondering how it all happened. Their nests gutted like the old mill itself. How terrible it must be to have no home.

All the chippings are all over the ground with long and terribly crooked beams. As I look the birds are looking too

at their roasted eggs lying terribly scarred and smashed
after the fiery flames of death.

Boy age 9.

A Dead Tree Root

It looks like a rough sea in storm,
It looks like a bird-eating spider,
It looks like a dinosaur with two legs and no head,
It looks like a long-dead chicken.
It feels crisp in my hand
And makes my palm tingle
As I touch little holes
Where something is pushing my finger away.
It is gnarled and creepy and beautiful
But it's ugly and horrid as well.

Boy age 10.

Dead Root

The surface of the root is like dry, raked soil
Or the fossil of a prehistoric animal.
When slowly moved it is all shapes
And is crispy and bulky to touch.
It is rough in the ridges and gnarled.
The colour is greeny blue
And flour-white with grey.
There are touches of yellow, orange and brown,
And it looks like a man's mouldy brain.

A Junior Boys' school of 203 pupils housed in the oldest Board
School building in a town of some 40,000 people. The parents and
grandparents of most of the children attended this school. Some of
the families live in the rows of back-to-back houses which adjoin
the school, others in blocks of new flats. Many of the mothers are
mill-workers.

The boys in my school have been unstreamed for the last six years.

*As I believe that it is only through creative experience that we really
learn, much work has been done through direct sensory experience which
nurtures the imagination of young children.*

Page 47

E

Such experience prompts speech which is allowed freedom whenever possible, this in turn allows writing that is rich and full of the child. I am not concerned, at this stage, with the form of the writing, only with the content. To this end feeding, so far as English is concerned, is from the great stories of literature, poems, legends, and folk tales from Genesis and Homer to Dylan Thomas and Ted Hughes. The many and varied experiences of the school all contribute to the quality of the written work, the many activities involving materials, the richness of P.E., drama and dance. The opportunity to experiment and to make and to talk freely of what is done, to discuss success and failure.

Though thoroughness and quality are demanded in many boys, the boys are not required to fit some adult pattern. They are yet juniors.

Boy age 10.

Our Street at Night

Night time falls over our street
The lamps shine down on the red brick houses
One or two weary workers clomp home
From a hard days work.
The blinds are down over the windows
At the co-op across the road.
From the fish-shop a delicious smell
Steals out into the night air.
David is crying
He has to go into bed.
A few cats stealthilly prowl around.
Bim an aged mongrel dog
Scratches the house door
Asking to be let in.
Whispy smoke rises
From the chimneys
As the night fires are lit.
There's Mrs. B . . .
Drawing her curtains
And turning her living room light on.
Suddenly the night silence is shattered
When Mr. S . . . booms off to work
On his blooming motor bike.

He works on the night shift
At Ardsley pit.
On push bikes,
Motor bikes,
In cars,
Or just walking
The youth group set out for home.
The silence falls
And it is as if our street
Has fallen asleep.

Boy age 10.

Escape

In a smoky closet two fags were burning. Smoke coming
out of two mouths puffing away.

Someone coming up the stairs!

Open the window. Die the fags out. Waft the smoke out
of the window . . . All's clear.

"Steven, Ian what are you doing?"

"Tidying the bedroom up, down in a minute."

"Have you been smoking?"

"No, Mam."

Boy age 10.

Our Street at Night

At six o'clock our neighbour comes home
And if she catches you on her garden
You have had it
The children make a noise
Theve to get ready for bed
There is a lonely house across the road
Polish people live in it
Houses have been pulled down around them
But they won't let the Corporation
Pull theirs down.
If you go on that land
They'll bawl and shout at you.

They think they own the land.
At half past seven on Wednesday
The noise seems to fade
I know why
Coronation Street is on the television
There's a policeman on our road every hour
Coronation Street is smashing
Except when Mr. M . . . uses his electric razor
Our street is quiet
Except at night
Then the lorry drivers pull up at the pub or fish shop
W . . .'s is the noisiest place
Wagons are cranked up,
You can never get to sleep
Until the noise stops.
When the equipment lorries pass to go to the Ace Products
The house shakes
There is Morley low Station near us
When a train goes into the station
You could hear the noise a mile off.
Our Graham never gets to sleep
He goes to the window every time a train comes,
Until he gets tired of this and goes to sleep.

Boy age 10.

My First Day in Mr. W . . .'s Class

That first day was awful. Everybody was doing a job, some washing paint-palletes, others tidying cupboards and I was helping to sort out books and put them in racks on the wall.

I did not think there was any point in it. I felt lost.

Mr. W . . . told P . . . to get some test tubes out of a box and put them in some kind of holders. But P . . . was clumsy and slipped on a book that someone had dropped. Crash, two test-tubes splintered into little fragments.

The teacher flew into a terrible rage, his face went red with anger, he shouted and bawled at P . . . , calling names like dolt, idiot, twerp, nit and twit. P . . . went white. I was quite nervous. Sometimes I fidgetted, I'm slightly below average height.

By play-time we had finished the jobs, and was I glad!

Boy age 9.

Why I Am Forgetful

Well, it's caused by the brain. I think it's the live part of the brain forgetting. Scientists might know what causes it but I don't. Anyway, I forgot football, although I like football really. It's because when I was at home I was hurrying as usual. Because I was lazy. I got out of bed late and then I forgot my tie. I could not be bothered to put it on. Then I dodged out of doing my hair but decided to be tidy and so I combed my hair. Recently Mr. T . . . sent me on an errand and I had to go back because I forgot what to say.

Boy age 10.

A Happy Day

The alarm clock rang out loudly, I looked up, it was 5 a.m. That day I was happy I was going with my Dad for the first time in his lorry.

Taking about 2 minutes to get dressed I rushed down-stairs. My Dad was already up. The light stung my eyes as I looked at my Dad. He was filling the flask with some tea. I went to get the sandwiches. My Dad had cheese sandwiches and I had sardines. Whilst I put my coat on the dog was chained by my Dad. A few minutes later we were in the car and on our way to work. 16 was the number of my Dad's lorry. The cab was too high for me to get into so I was lifted by my Dad. I was so excited that I forgot to ask where we were going — but I needn't have done because my Dad said, "We are off to Newcastle and then to Rotherham."

A burring noise came to my ears as my Dad started the engine. I saw an orange cloth behind the drivers seat so I said "Is that cloth to wipe the windows with?" "Yes you can wipe them if you want", he answered. It was all so thrilling the fields just whizzed past and when we went down a hill they went even faster by. A few hours past but they only seemed like minutes, and we were passing an aerodrome. I said, "Can we stop and watch the aeroplanes?" but my father said, "There won't be any planes flying for a bit, but we'll stop when we are on our way back." After looking out of the window for a bit I felt sleepy and eventually I dropped off to sleep. The next thing I knew we were at Newcastle.

The lorry was loaded and then we set out for home. Stopping at the aerodrome we saw four jets and two practise planes. On the way home we stopped at a cafe for a cup of tea and a bun. Eventually the lorry pulled into the garage and we were back. A few minutes we were home. Everything had been so exciting that day. I had been with my Dad and his Lorry for the first time.

Boy age 10.

Autumn Day

Today the air is cool and there is a slight breeze to comfort it.

The reck is slightly damp with footprints and tyre-marks, some worn and some fresh. Some ponies are grazing with the sun's glaring heat on their backs. Here the ground has stony muddy puddles on it. Some people are washing their flags to get the mud off. We are nearing a stream. This stream starts from an old pipe and the water is foamy and murky. Under the water is water slime and scores of water shrimps. Farther on I saw some elderberry bushes and a small hut with pebbles outside and lots of daisies.

Work from a school of 302 Junior Boys and Girls from a typical South Yorkshire mining area. The school was "unstreamed" three years ago but most of the pupils whose writing is quoted were in the last of the streamed classes.

Much time and effort are given in the endeavour to develop a child's ability in English. We must ask ourselves — is our effort in the right direction and is our time purposefully used?

Children learn to write by writing and writing creatively. What they need is opportunity. English exercises, studies in words and in simple grammar can never be substitutes for creative writing. Again, why work up something special for "composition" when there are so many interests? Children need a teacher who can use their real and varied experiences, experiences of their environment, emotion and imagination. They need one who can help them to see things more vividly, to feel more intensely; one who can maintain their powers of perception through constant stimulation. Confidence and encouragement play an important part in creative activity. The child needs confidence in his own ability to succeed and encouragement to strive for greater success. Success engenders success, and here encouragement is of the greatest value.

Imagination is of prime importance. Foster the imagination — for this unique channel provides for expression of the deeper self. Its development cannot be too strongly emphasised. It exerts a great influence that makes for individual growth and allows the child to be capable of living and developing at his maximum.

Girl age 10.

The Candle

White polish; sour milk.
Delicate finger wrapped in cotton blanket.
Star growing, bigger, bigger flickering in darkness,
A great Lord, now a humble person bowing.
Golden crystals, dark eye,
Slowly, flowing, running, milk.
Faint glimmer of hope, trying to enlarge itself.
Black burned pie; all beauty gone.

Girl age 11.

Snowball Fight

Whizzing snowballs like Pegasus soaring along. Shouts of Charge! Chaaaarge!. Snowballs like hand grenades, and when they hit you that's the explosion going off. Faces like ruby rings, in a shop window, and blooming roses. The third years are a weed in the top years garden and they must be hacked out or killed off with snowballs. The bell for coming in goes straight through one ear and comes out the other, teachers fling open windows shouting, "Come on troops".

Boy age 10.

Bolton and It's Surroundings

The school stands out against other houses and buildings because it is surrounded by green lawns and a large field. Groups of semi-detached houses look like toy buildings against big green and yellow fields.

The fields spread around engulfing towns like a whirlpool swallows up a log while the road looks like a slow moving river rolling onwards towards Highgate and Goldthorpe.

The fields wave to and fro up hills and down low valleys. Partridges and pheasants, hares and rabbits and even foxes roam these fields.

But towns are fast growing and soon they will replace the vast fields and spreading woodlands.

The Power station at Mexborough looks like an enormous battery of guns piping shells and smoke skywards.

Boy age 10.

Our Street

There is one person who I don't like in our street. They call her Mrs. A . . . . On March the 7th. I was playing football with my friend Michael. He kicked the ball high and I jumped to head it. I fell to the ground and cut my lip so I started spitting down the grate, to get the blood out of my mouth. Out came Mrs. A . . ., with her two dogs, she said, "First its the racket now its the ball. Get up there and play". Two minutes later Mr. A . . . came out and said "What have you been spitting at my Mrs. for

John?" I said "I havn't been spitting at your Mrs. If you don't believe me look down the grate". He looked down the grate and went in.

To say Mrs. A . . . has lived in the street least she has done most complaining.

Boy age 11.

The Balloon

Bright leaves, Nature's pride and joy
Slender innocence,
   Hanging like rain on the bought.
Then, like a burst pipe expanding, lung-like
   Aerobatic displays, bounding on air,
Hovering feats of twisting.
   Then a child's heart is broken,
Nothing can replace it.

Boy age 10.

My Village — Bolton-on-Dearne

A large common village with common people, friendly people and unfriendly people. Lovely sweet green grass surrounding a wonderful school. Television ariels crowding and cluttering the chimney pots. A life of television. Cats and dogs barking and screeching. A busy and bustling village in parts and quiet and inanimate in others. I like Bolton in some ways and hate it in others. I love its cool shady trees. I hate its winding dirty road.

Boy age 10.

Bolton and Its Surroundings

As I look south I see a crowd of dull black smoking chimney pots. I see the drooping willow tree leaning over the fence shedding tears to water the fields that have been dry for over a week.

In the distance you can see a cluster of little old houses which are surrounded by beautiful lawns and flowers or some with sheds and greenhouses.

Far away in the west you can see the houses of Wombwell. Not far from there you can see the Barnsley Road with all the people rushing to the shops to spend their wages, and then there is the traffic whizzing by, the road is always busy, from a distance they look like flies crawling up the wall.

Round a lot of fields are bushes separating one field from another.

Boy age 10.

Trains

The chugging and hollow clanking of the old steam engine sounds quite like the hammering and banging of a busy hard working steel factory. As it slowly drags and pulls its heavy caterpillar like train, I sit looking through the smoke blackened window, sometimes hills and lakes pass, frightenings an unwary rabbit or a soot black crow perching on the fence. Still trees suddenly spring back to life in the gusts of wind. As the sun parched body of the giant engine passes through the abandoned broken down railway station it lurches to a halt.

Boy age 11.

Frost

Grey clouds, puffing out of chimneys,
mingling with the sky's bulking ribs.
Gleaming hoar, sparkling diamonds,
staring the sun in the face.
Stiff, crisp, the brittle green bars,
imprison sunlight.

Boy age 10.

Thinking

Lorries and cars roam up and down the hill like jet planes taking off on a busy run way. The playground is half wet and half dry blotches of black show where puddles have soaked into the asphalt.

Everything seems quiet except for the shuffling of feet and chairs.

The pipes are cold.

The weather is cold.

The wind blows cold thoughts into my mind.

Everything is cold.

The pictures on the wall seem to move with the wind.

The trees and flowers nearly quake their heads off in the cool shivering wind.

The lamp posts stand towering above us, they seem to bow their heads down to the cars as they come whizzing by.

From a small rural Junior Mixed and Infants school with a little over 100 children on roll. It is a four-teacher school with more than one age group in each class. The children are drawn mainly from mining and mill working families.

Creative writing was treated as an art form and much writing was done each day. The two essentials we thought our writing must possess were sensitivity and sincerity.

Without sensitivity the child will be unable to make an experience really his own. It is obvious that to develop this sensitivity the child must be given many opportunities to use his different senses and his attention must occasionally be focused on one particular aspect of the experience in order that his sensitivity may be deepened as well as widened.

There must also be sensitivity in the use of words, so that the child is encouraged to search his own vocabulary for the right word. A great deal of this vocabulary is built up by his reading, both in and out of school, and from other sources such as T.V. It is the teacher's task not to provide the words for this vocabulary, but to build up an interest in words by which the child will take words and make them his own.

Sincerity is even more important. It is relatively easy for a child, especially an able child, to write something which has a superficial brilliance without any core of real experience. The basis of creative writing is that a child should be able to write about an experience in such a way that having given expression to his feelings the experience becomes more meaningful for him, and in this way helps to deepen his imaginative powers. This does not mean that a child writes only for himself. By sharing his experience with others it becomes more significant for all. For this he must have the right words, and he will be encouraged to find these in the hope that by so doing his communication will become that much clearer.

Girl age 6.

> In the market on monday morning
> It is busy as busy can be. With laughing
> And shouting and scremeing from end to
> End. With clanging and banging and
> Wanging. On pottery stores. Up and down
> Round about. Up the full and dirt streets.
> The dustmans van came lumbering down
> Bumpety, Bumpety Bump the cars came rackiling
> Down the street chacl chacl chacl I
> Never got use to the market on monday
> mandy morning.

Girl age 10.

The Bear with a Million Fleas

In a forest not far away from Nottingham there lived a handsome bear. He was kind willing and wise, but there was one thing wrong he had a tremendous amount of fleas. The other bears dare not go near him for fear of catching them. One day the bear was walking through the wood when he saw a monkey. The monkey was scratching "What are you scratching for"?. said the Bear. "Oh I have fleas," The bear answered "so have I and I cant get rid of them. How on earth do you catch them. I've always been clean. Do you want to get rid of yours"? "Of course I do" said the monkey. I know lets get rid of them together." So the monkey and the bear set off together to get rid of their fleas. They came to river. I know said the bear we will jump in the river, and get rid of our fleas. So the bear jumped in then the monkey and they both drowned.

Girl age 9.

Voices in the Mist

A blanket of mist lay above the town of Sedminster, round about the time 9 o'clock. I crept down the dismal street towards the centre of the town, feeling a little scared of every minute to come. Then I realized there was nothing to be scared of, but I could not be sure, anything could be behind me that I did not know of. I heard sweet, but faint voices singing as if they were saying something to me. Feeling more frightened I wondered whether to go on or turn back. I thought to myself was I imagining things or could I really hear voices, but I didn't know so the question still remained. In the distance I could see a very faint light which came from, or what I thought came from a house. But I was wrong, when I drew nearer it was a church and a choir practising for the Sunday service. So I walked on and had nothing to be afraid of.

Boy age 9.

A Night Walk

I am walking silently along a windy lane, the trees are rustling in the midnight breeze. I can hear a faint ripple it is coming from that ditch across the road as if a pipe was leaking and spreading everywhere. Whats that? its only the bracken crackling as I tred on it. I can hear a croaking sound like a grasshopper but I think it is a miller working late. The moon is coming slowing out and lighting up the earth. There is a leaf near me blowing in the breeze, it is now crackling as I tread on it with my big heavy shoes. The trees are waving the branches as if to say good by to a friend. The moons face is like a African boys face who has caught a disease and warts have come on his face to ruin his skin. A dark veil of cloud is creeping over the moon, as I crossed the bridge I hung over the river. I seemed to be walking endlessly through space where the footpath never ends. I stopped and leaned over the edge of the bridge and I saw the moon come slowly out from behind the veil of darkened cloud. Suddenly I heard a splash and I run on towards my house as I entered I heard a strange noise I rested when I saw it was the cat.

Girl age 10.

Rain

As I sat wondering one day by the window of our new house in Cardiff, I noticed something utterly new. The rain was falling lightly on the ground, gently passing the windows and suddenly the wind came. Of course I had seen rain many times before, but the funny thing was that before it had seemed like a common natural thing and on this particular day it was something quite different. It was like a lot of dancing girls who had just learned to dance. They were young and enthusiastic. Their tiny blocked shoes, their ribboned hair complete with frilly dresses made them look perfectly lovely. I had always wanted to be a ballarina and I really got carried away. The rain must have carried on for an hour or so. My mother called me and I came back to my senses to find that, Alas! It was nothing but plain simple grey rain!

Boy age 9.

The sea was calm and the sand was wet. The rocks were grey and covered with dark green sea weed that had come with the roaring tide small crabs scrambled over the rocks. There was a spectral mist over the sea. Now I could hear the water splashing in the caves and it echoed loudly, the sky was grey. There was a great roar of thunder and it began to rain. There were little rings of water on the ground. The sound was like some pebbles dropping on concrete the rain fell hard in the night But it soon became silent.

Boy age 9.

The Street at Night

The street at night is black as pitch with flickering stars of the gloomy sky. There is a sudden thunder as a car tears round the corner, it flashes by the street still on its journey. A pair of eyes suddenly stare at me from behind a group of old upturned boxes. It peers fiercely at me with its pointed ears. Then it disappears across the street and into the shadow by the lamp. The silent night goes on not pausing till the break of light, and the mornings work beginning. The night returns and the cat moves through the veil of darkness. The moon comes out, stars too, lamp comes on to light the darkened street. The branches of the trees rustle in the wind and an occasional leaf drops off the tree. Your hair blows back in the wind like the grass stuck to the ground.

Girl age 10.

The Rain Horse

The young man was walking over the hill when he felt the first drops of rain on his face. He hurried down to the wood in the middle of the valley and there he took refuge under a large twisting tree. He put up his collor and brought his knees up to his chest to keep out the cold. It was then that he saw the horse. It was black with a long mane, and it was stood upon the ridge, where the sky meets the hill tops. The sky was misty, for the night was drawing near and the black horse showed up beautifully against the pale gray.

The horse was only small, and after he had stood for a moment, it set off in a frantic gallop along the ridge and down the other side of the hill. He could not help but think of the horse, so he turned himself round and began studying the ways of the tree. He know this place, although not as well as he used to, because twelve years ago he had spent his childhood in the village two miles away. He came through these woods for quiet walks when he had done something wrong. He had let all these thoughts runaway with him, so he pulled himself together and began counting the rings on the bark, when suddenly he had a strange feeling. Someone was watching him! He did not dare move. Was it just because he was alone. NO! Someone was distinctly watching him.

A small Junior Mixed school in the worst part of a small industrial town. Most of the surrounding buildings consist of slum property which is slowly being cleared. Many of the better families in the area have moved to new housing estates and those left contain a fairly large proportion of problem families and less able children.

The main aim is to guide the children to express their own thoughts and feelings in a clear, logical and sensitive manner. In order to do this a great deal of the work of the school is adapted to give the child as much opportunity as possible of showing his individuality, creativeness, sensitivity and awareness. Children are taught as individuals and the teachers aim to give their children the opportunity to show these qualities and to have confidence in themselves. Each child has, in our opinion, the power to do something well and this is encouraged and used as a jumping off ground. No child is regarded as backward. The carry-over from one subject to another is exploited as much as possible, for once the children gain confidence in themselves progress in every way seems automatic.

The recalling of past experiences and observation and awareness of things around them is continually encouraged and in this way their interests are kept vital and fresh. Because of repeated sensory experiences which are obtained in lessons such as movement and drama, the study of the world around, Art, Music, and Poetry, the children express themselves in language which is alive, direct and colourful. The language they express themselves in is sincere and direct, lacking artificiality and sophistication. Throughout all written and oral work there is an obvious delight in the sound and selection of words.

The reading of the children's own work to other children, followed by discussion and constructive criticism, is another feature of the written work which helps to keep the work alive. The use of books of exercises is not encouraged and the rules of Grammar and Spelling are taken as the opportunity occurs but no formal instruction in Grammar and Spelling is given.

Girl age 11.

Someone I Know

He has light grey hair with a bald patch on top. He puts grease on and tries to make it stick down but it never works.

His skin is very brown and swarthy. He likes the country and most of all to go fishing on a red hot day. Every time I see him he has a cigarette or a pipe in his mouth. He also likes looking after poultry and pigs, and he has an allotment where he grows some beautiful flowers.

I like to be in his company, he is a very talkative person and you can not get a word in edge-ways when he is speaking to you. He never borrows anything from anybody but he always lends his things out. He always has a brown suit and a brown trilby. His eyes are like blue pins and they flash when he is mad. His eyebrows are bushy and you can see where a scar runs through because they part. You can not see his eyelashes because they are very fair. He is tall and thin he has high cheek bones and his chin seems to come to a point at the end. When ever I go to their house he always buys me sweets he is very kind. The person I know is my uncle Goerge.

Girl age 11.

Floods

Rain just continuous rain I heard, "Floods," the word caught my ear as my father came in. I went down to Castleford to see what the river was like and saw that it was not far from the bridge. Sand bags were round nearly all the grates. Water was rushing round the cars and as they drove madly, through the swirling water is splashed against my face.

What was the difference in the weather? Then I suddenly noticed that the rain had stopped. I was angry because it started to slow down and suddenly it stopped, and just as soon as it had stopped it started again. It began to rain faster and faster. How pleased and excited I was but what if somebody was drowned? I was afraid as well as excited as this thought rushed through my mind. How cold my feet were! As the water went into my shoe I shivered as each step I took more water seeped into my shoe which squelshed as I walked. It was interesting to watch the water come through holes in them. Next day the rain ceased and the water slowly disappeared.

Girl age 11.

My Own Poem About the Snow
The snow came gently falling
  With its flakes dancing and twirling,
Its rays shining and glistning,
  Gently it falls.

You touch it
  And it is soft white velvet,
Cold as ice,
  As beautiful as peacock feathers.
Slowly it reaches the ground
  Settles there
And quietly sleeps.

Boy age 11.

The Riverside
So calm is the river as the clouds float overhead. How soft the sandbank looks and feels under me as it stretches down to the water. Look, there is a sand martin stretching its wings in the sand, so soft and cool. Further over the sand we look to the flat open fields where herds of cows are grazing. Then our eye catches the river gleaming in the sunlight, with the little Roach bobbing up and down and disturbing the water. Here I have some weed, how smooth it feels, it is very shiny. The smell reminds me of the sea air.

Boy age 11.

The Proud Newt
The Newt is a lizard-like reptile which has small delicate little feet.

I remember when it was brought to school and how it wriggled when somebody picked it up. I remember also how it used to sit on its rock proudly and lordly, and if it was disturbed it would dart back into the water and stealthily creep back when all was quiet again.

Girl age 11.

My Own Poem
Snowflakes

Down Down the snow came,
Filling the cracks and crevices of the black roads,
   Swiftly blowing against trees,
Giving them a coat of dazzling snow,
And crunching beneath my feet.

   So silent and quiet,
The sharp pointed icicles hung by the brown walls,
Catching the light and glittering like,
Rubies and sapphires and emeralds,
Against the dark little town.

Never stopping and whirling and dancing,
Covering houses and people and trees,
The Snowflakes came falling and falling
And my colour blind eyes watched as they fell.

Boy age 11.

From a berry to a tree
Is like a child to a man
It grows, and grows till reaches the sky
And it is larger than you and I.

With its great dark trunk
And its small bright leaves
It twinkles and gleams in the winter eves
And is a lovely sight to see.

Work from an unstreamed Junior Mixed school of 265 children. The pupils come from council and private estates; most of them are from working-class homes, though some are the children of professional or business men. About half the children are expected to do reasonably well on a more academic secondary school course, but those who come from the slum-clearance areas are educationally impoverished and need much help from the school.

We believe the enjoyment of books and good literature are essential for good written English. There is a large and varied collection of books in the school which the children are encouraged to use at all times of the day. Children's classics and good modern stories are frequently read aloud to the children as well as a great deal of poetry.

The children's powers of observation are developed in all branches of school work and we aim to give the children many varied experiences. Usually they choose the subjects they wish to write about. We try to help them to appreciate language and to write imaginatively as well as factually. No books of English exercises are used, as this seems to kill lively written English.

We often read to the older children excerpts from adult books, especially biographies such as Richard Church's "Over the Bridge", where childhood experiences are vividly described. This helps them to be more aware of their own experiences and sensitive and vivid accounts of some episode in their own lives often results.

Only a small proportion of the work is corrected. As the enjoyment of books and fluency in writing develops there is little need for the correction of work done by the more able children. With the younger as well as with the less intelligent children we aim to correct as much work as possible individually with the child beside us.

No formal grammar is taught but individual children or groups of children are made aware of grammatical mistakes.

However, I am coming to the conclusion that the more intelligent children in the last year of the Junior school would enjoy and be capable of understanding the intricacies of some English grammar.

Boy age 7.

Snow in the Woods
As it was snowing at the edge of a wood
A little old man and a donkey stood
A little old hat and a stick so small
A little brown coat and a big white shawl.

The donkey grey with a saddle brown
To keep himself warm walked up and down
The fields were white and the trees were bare
Along came a rabbit and a big big hare.

They searched for food but found none there
So the little old man fed the rabbit and hare.

Boy age 7.

My Mother

My Mother has brown hair green eyes and somtimes she has a green jumper. She is a bit of a bossyboots even if we do some of the housework. Sometimes she buys us sweets and comics if we're good. When my mother washes my jeans I always say they wont be dry for morning. She smokes cigeretes but I say the smoke is getting in my eyes. My mother is very patient and waits for things. She is always smoking and I get board watching my mum smoke. She wasts her money on them I say she ought to stop it but once you get in the habbit you cant get out of it.

Girl age 11.

The View from the Top of Carr Lane

Sunshine catches a window near Spring Wood. It is a cool breezy day today. A church spire stands out from the many factories and houses. The spire is a dull grey but even so it stands out better then anything else. One of the many double decker buses climbs slowly up Carr Lane. At each stop it sounds as if it cannot go on. Two white houses stand alone in the streets of grey smoke covered houses. The sun shines through a dirty grey cloud on to the maze of fields. Towering above the other buildings is a clock with four spires on the flat top of it. Smoke curls round a tall round factory chimmeny near the market square. The square looks very clean with its red roads compared with the rest of Shipley. Some washing is blowing wildly about in the breeze. The smoke from an unseen house comes up from behind a hill. A train chugs along gathering speed. Don't you think its a lovely view from the top of Carr Lane.

Boy age 9.

Nativity Poem

In the old old days,
And poor poor ways.
Jesus was born
In a poor and meek old barn.
But he was to be the king of the Jews,
And he never did lose,
His fight.

When the shepherds came,
And saw him where he lay,
They thanked God in prayer,
For Jesus upon the hay.
And gave him a present,
A present, a little lamb.

The three wise men came from afar,
Melchior, Gaspar, Balthazar.
Melchior bringing Gold,
Gaspar Frankincens to bring,
And Balthazar bringing Myrrh
For the King.

Boy age 9.

A Pirate

The pirate was peering through a long slender telescope and was sitting with his foot upon the capstan. He had a long grey beard that met his shoulders, and a narrow clay pipe with curls of smoke rising up from it. He had a patch over his eye and a wooden peg-leg. His yellow trousers and red waistcoat showed up very brightly against the dirty grey deck of the galleon. However it did not show up as much as a great scar on the right side of his forehead.

He had a long chin with a greyish white beard growing from it, which made laughter arise from among the pirates. I could see his face was brown with the boring hot sun. The pirate had no shoes on, and his toe nails were dirty and needed cutting. He was very proud of his yellow trousers, which came down to his knees.

Boy age 10.

Spring

Here comes spring,
The skylarks sing
Here comes spring again
No drifts of snow down the lane
Now that spring has come again
Now that all the snow is gone
Listen to the birds sweet song
Listen to sparrows sing.

Boy age 11.

The Day of the Fire

One day I was walking down a lane, when I heard a clanging noise, and I saw a fire engine rumbling up the lane. It swept by, and as it dissapeared I wondered where the fire was. I hurried on, and I eventually came to a big cornfield. It was a blazing fire, so that the grass, which was black, showed through the leaping flames. The dry corn crackled and smoked. Men were standing by, and I recognised one of them as the owner of the field. He stood looking dolefully at the brilliant crimson and vermilion flames. Grey smoke curled up from the fire. Smartly dressed firemen held hose-pipes to the fire. The water spouted like a million glittering diamonds into the termoil of smoke and fire. Gradually the fire waned until only a few lingering flames remained. It was a pityfull scene. All the grass was black and desolate, and wisps of smoke curled up into the air where a few minutes earlier there had been a raging angry blaze of smoke and flame. I walked thoughtfully away, down the lane, to the everyday scene of traffic and houses, which all seemed so different from the fire in the cornfield. Excitedly I related my experience to my mother and father when I got home.

Boy age 11.

Icicles

Hanging from the porch
Are slippery white icicles.
Gone the suns scorch,
Now the frosts bite.

They hang there pointed and long,
Now, only now that summer has gone.
Transparent and cold, over the porch they hang low,
Through ice and cold winds,
through winter and snow.

Softly, white icicles float from the sky,
Cold and hard hang icicles,
white with silver sheen,
Now the winter has come and warm summer has been.

Girl age 11.

Holy Tuesday

It shocked me to think that Jesus was going back to the Temple after the events of Monday. He had made a lot of enemies. I could not believe that anyone could possibly hate Jesus. In the Temple his enemies tried to trap him by asking trick questions. Of course they failed. Once more Jesus was victorious. Through all this Jesus had remained calm. Later on that day Jesus took us up to the Mount of Olives. It was very quiet, a long way away from everyone. Jesus told us that he would die and rise again in words we did not understand then. He told us a lot about what was going to happen. His voice sounded sad which made me unhappy too. Jesu's words rang through my mind. When he said that he had many enemies I felt puzzled.

I knew he could defend himself against them if he wanted to. But would he want to? This was the thought that was worrying me. As I was thinking I suddenly felt ashamed. Jesus would do the right thing I was certain. With this thought I smiled to myself. I was a lot happier.

Work from a school of 260 Junior Boys and Girls, now in its third year. The school is streamed by age, not ability. About 14 per cent of the pupils are children of professional and clerical workers, the rest of manual workers, skilled and unskilled.

Principles and practice

We consider the needs of the child, and endeavour to place him in a situation where he has the opportunity to fulfil these needs. We encourage him to communicate and express himself in movement and words, and through Art, Music, etc. He talks and writes about his environment. Sometimes his teacher takes him out and makes him aware of something in the wood, for example, or an incident in or around school, and the child writes or paints about it immediately (as a primary experience). At other times the teacher builds up knowledge from his own experience, from Literature, Poetry or other sources, and the child may be asked to write about this (secondary experience), e.g. the teacher may read poems about the gipsies, may discuss a painting of a gipsy caravan, etc., and then ask the child to write about "A day in the life of a gipsy". On other occasions, the child may be shown something for the experience alone and we hope that this will enrich future work. We believe that this writing from past experience brings the best imaginative work.

Teachers also read to the children, and each child is expected to retell the story in his own words. Sometimes he is asked to extend the story and write from his imagination. Often, of course, the teacher reads to the child for the love of literature, with no intention of asking the child to write.

At other times the child is expected to write freely on any given title or topic, e.g. "Fire", "Lost", etc., to write about the pets they bring and the people they know.

Comprehension exercises, grammar, etc.

When planning for the school opening in 1960, I bought one set for each age group, of books containing English Exercises. This was in case any teachers were against the methods I intended to use. I am happy to say that these books have been used only on very rare occasions. We find that by far the best results are obtained from the correction of the child's own work. Imaginative work, and work resulting from a primary experience, are read by the teacher, but not marked for grammatical errors unless the child is present. Corrections and teaching points are extracted from retelling stories, when the child has not to think so much about the content.

It is important to remember that we expect a good standard from the children, that the senses of the children are always being awakened, and that Movement, Music and Art all help towards good written work.

Girl age 9.

Outside Today

The first time I set my foot outside the wind surrounded me in coldness. We ran onto the grass. Blades of grass was covered in dew. It looked like a thousand diamonds, sparkling when the sun caught them. When I looked to the woods it was a different picture. The trees stood big and strong, as if to say "Keep out of this wood, we own it!" The background which was light was the paper, the trees were the picture. As my eyes wandered up to the sky, one part of the sky was moving lazily. It looked as though it had just been swept with a brush. We slowly walked back to our classroom. My feet were in misery when we came in.

Girl age 10.

A Windy Day

I know that in the poem of the year it says "March brings breezes loud and shrill" but I don't think we had a breeze today. It was a blundering, heavy, noisy wind. The wind blew my dress up till I could see the pimples on my skin. Once I put it down it would be up again in a minute. When I turned my back on this fearful wind it seamed as though I was turning my back on all my worries. The wind hit my back as if it was crashing in to a wall. Then finding that there was no way through the wall "that was my back", it stopped and let it self round the side. Then another blow of wind would come and do the same as the first one. The wind blew all the twigs. As the clouds blew across the sky the bit of sun there was kept getting hidden. Because of that the grass and the land around went dark then light again. It was as if day and night were in fast motion. When the wind roaghed it sounded like a gient practising singing and trying also to hold it on.

Boy age 10.

Our Visit to the Gramer School

As I looked through the network of wire netting at the deserted trees there came a sudden hope for spring. The sun shone warmly on my neck. The sky was made up of happy blues and solemn greys. When we got to the Grammar school, there was the sqeal of the thing they use to put up the scaffolding with. Then there was the skeleton temple. A man walked up to it and put up a ladder between one of its bones, and walked up to the top of the temple with greatest confidence hands in pocket pipe in mouth, he walked around on the skeleton roof.

The massive crater was deserted and forlorn. It was like ghost town. Not even a mouse stirred in that place. The house of either worm or a spider which ever it was I don't know but it must have snuggled up in bed. Before the workmen were swarming all over like ants now nobody seemed botherd. The ground seemed hard and rugged. At the other side of the works, you could hear the compresor chugging like an old car. the crane stood moitness the trees stood bare and forgotton.

Girl age 10.

A White World

Shuffling feet, and chattering teeth. Complete silence except the faint sound of traffic.

The grass was like a frozen lake of ice, on top of the ice there appeared to be a thousand grains of salt. Nothing was visible in the pale heavens. The school lights twinkled in the distance. When I walked over the grass it was crisp. Patches of green showed through the frost, and the field resembled a green and white mosaic floor. One blade of grass was long and slender, it had little balls of frost gently clinging to it. The fog hovered around wood. The dark motionless trees stood high and mighty. One of the trees was like a feathery beard. Little puffs of cotton wool sprinkled allover. A web was set upon the bark of a tree, it was light and delicate. When I got to the playground I turned to look at the wood but only the fog was visible.

Boy age 10.

My Pets

Eeny and Meeny, my two hedgehogs wobbled across the short, newly cut grass. They looked like old veteran cars, rocking from side to side. When they where in a ball they look like black pincushions with hundreds of black and white pins the wrong way round in them. They were about a month old, but they had very sharp spines. They looked very cute even though they are called the pigs of the hedge. When I put some milk out for them, the milk seems to evaporate up their noses. Sometimes their eyes seemed to glisten even though they are partly coverd by fur. You could hardly see their small ears because of the long fur round its face.

Boy age 9.

Enormous huge our hall is in size, and in width, it has a dangerous feeling for me in the hall. We were in assembly when the windows began to shake and creak and it was dangerous, it might have fallen in. But we carried on, his voice rang out, then we sang, it rang out all round the hall. Mr. . . . took it that day, we said our prayers it was soundless. Then the window began to shake and creak more and more until we went out. It was a big lonely hall I think.

Girl age 10.

Lost!

The wind moaned and the sky shook. Torents of rain lashed upon the dry parched earth. Trees bowed down to the mighty storm. Gradully the rain ceased and the wind faded away. Every thing was still. The sun made a feeble atempt to shine. A wood pigeon slowly circled, then carefully landed on a gnarled branch. From the dephs of the forest came an agonising wail. A small rabbit was trapped in a rabbit snare. He was an albino. The rabbit had wandered away from his burrow, and now he was lost. There he lay without a hope of survival. The pain was agonising. It was fighting against hunger and death. A scratch then a kick, the rabbit lay motionless. The next time the rabbit opened his eyes he was in a small hutch. Soft warm straw was piled around him. A saucer of milk lay near his feet, spherical and sweet. The rabbit closed his eyes, knowing that he would never fear anything again.

WORK FROM FOUR SECONDARY SCHOOLS
(TWO MODERN AND TWO GRAMMAR)

From a three-form-entry Girls' Modern school in a mining area.
Ample opportunity is given for practice in Written English throughout the school. The basis of the work is a thorough knowledge of good Literature. Whatever a pupil writes about someone has written about before her, and when the teacher knows where to look for parallels to the child's experience the child is helped to discover the joys of Literature. The children have the experience of (a) listening to good prose and poetry being read aloud in a sensitive way and (b) of reading the best themselves. If the girls are to write about a pirate, then we feel we must set before them lots of examples from Literature, e.g. the pirate from "The Green Dolphin Country", the "Treasure Island" pirate and pirates from poetry. They do need this experience and to this they add their own.

We allow everyone to experiment with words and the use of words. Every word must mean something. This knowledge of words banishes doggerel in poetry and the extravagant use of similes in prose. We encourage girls to use their eyes and their ears — to use their five senses. We ask them to look out of the window, to look for details in people, animals and objects and to listen to sounds. This is done informally. We experiment with words through Speech and Drama, through Poetry and Written English. It is interesting to note that the girls who can compose poetry and write good descriptive prose can also record their facts clearly and concisely. In this way the girls are encouraged to use their Mother Tongue freely and logically in both spoken and written English.

Apart from the G.C.E. work we do not give formal instruction in Grammar, but there is an abundance of individual guidance. The girl must discover where she is wrong and put it right. The greatest difficulty we find is the question of incomplete sentences and this we find can only be cured through sensible reading and individual attention. There is always something about which one can write and, with the co-operation of the staff, the teachers of English help the child to find the subject. The research, the practical work, the recording and the arranging give the girls a wide experience of many subjects hitherto considered rather boring.

Girl age 15.

Chancing Our Luck

Blackpool has always been one of Britain's most popular holiday resorts. The moment holiday-makers arrived their first thought was — the beach, but nowadays the minute they step off the train they tread the well-worn path of fools to the bingo parlours. Bingo has swept the country off its feet. Even songs have been written about it. The homely inn on the corner of the street where the village statesman used to exchange their views and stale news and even older jokes were passed round now lies deserted. "Clickety-click" and "legs eleven" have taken all their trade.

Foreigners often talk of the "casinos" of the continent! They should come to our country. Britain is one huge cauldron of casinos. No-one seems to think anything against putting his shirt on "Lady Luck". We are now one of the greatest gambling nations in the world — if not the greatest. Horses tempt us as perfume tempts a Frenchman.

Indeed, a basket of crumpled betting slips could be a symbol of society's new freedom and affluence . . . or its emptiness.

An inconspicuous little weed of a man comes to town in early spring and buys a broken down, incongruous, poky, little shop. The next day he bangs up a notice over the door bearing his name and the words "Licensed Betting Office", written in uneven writing and in an unbecoming shade of brown. People queue up for their "rations" of the Derby, day after day, day after day.

By Christmas, the ugly duckling little man who walked into the shop, walks out in his fifty guinea suit towards his chauffeur-driven Rolls Royce car, cigar in hand, an expanse of "tum" where his ribs once protruded his flesh, relishing in the anticipation of his visit to his favourite, film-star girlfriend.

Fairs used to be places where Romeo used to show off to his sweetheart how hard he could punch a leather ball hanging from a chain. He used to put his arm protectingly around her as they came whooshing down the big dipper together. Fancy-free young girls would buy candy-floss and toffee apples as they tripped gaily about the fair admiring every eligible Adonis. Now they all stand in a circle feeding gluttonous one-armed bandits and fruit machines with pennies and sixpences, their faces as cheerful as if they were standing in silent prayer.

At Church garden parties one used to spend money by paying about sixpence to enter a race, the winner receiving an enjoyable prize or paying a fee to see the parish treasures. That is all changed; everything is in competition form. One pays to guess at the number of logs in a pile, the number of peas in a jar and even the height of the church tower.

Some greyhound tracks, in the name of sport, are becoming dens of cruelty. In the afternoon before a big race the trainer lets a tame rabbit loose and lets the greyhound after it. Sometimes the rabbit has scarcely gone ten yards when the greyhound grabs it and with a vicious shake of the head breaks its neck. The greyhound is then allowed to continue to maul it and greedily licks up the still alive rabbit's warm blood. After the meal the greyhound licks its lips in the luxuriance of having tasted blood. At some grounds tame rabbits are fastened to the mechanical hares to make the dog run. Once a dog has tasted blood it keeps wanting more and therefore runs when it can smell an animal that it is able to kill.

One can almost compare a greyhound's lust for blood to a human's desire to "chance his luck".

Girl age 15.

From a composition entitled "A Cathedral City"

The sirens had gone. The worst was to come, a slight drone was heard like the buzz of a bee, before gently landing on some unsuspecting flower. As the drone became more intense, faces in underground passages and sheds became gripped with fear. Mouths moved but no words came out. Children sat glued to their mothers' aprons. Some were asleep with blissful smiles lighting up their smutty faces, others had faces screwed up like an old newspaper as they sat rigid waiting for the climax. It was near. Suddenly it came as expected but it still shocked. Just when it seemed as if the ear drums would burst the huge, terrifying bangs came. The forcibly darkened streets burst into light, flickering and eating everything which lay in its path, its huge fangs licking round the buildings, as its yellow teeth gnawed at the woodwork. The raid was on, bombs were dropped and the streets were on fire.

In the morning, out of the shelters and passages the people of Coventry came to see desolation. The familiar roads and streets, their homes, their factories, and their public buildings were gone. All that symbolised that a town was once there were the piles of smoking rubble in which the homeless were scratching and scrambling to try and find some part of their home which was not destroyed. A photograph of a husband or son could bring hope and something to live for in the lives of those lost citizens.

After the shock of not being able to find a home, the people noticed something strange in the skyline of the city. Where were the spire, the bells, the carved masonry, the stained glass windows and the sound of organ music and chanting choirs? The cathedral was down in the rubble to be trampled on with the rest of the common buildings but there was inspiration. Part of a wall still remained and someone had erected two crosses, one made of the charred beams, the other of three huge nails, as old as the cathedral itself. These were to become the marks or symbols of Coventry and to major cities of the world nail crosses were sent out to show what war had done to Coventry.

Girl age 15.

From a composition entitled "A Railway Station"

The day was cool but the two comfortable waiting rooms conveyed no sign of emptiness so I was content to keep the train's company.

The large, red buffers placed at the end of the line looked like a mechanical freak with two frightening eyes. Enough to stop any locomotive, no matter how powerful. A long, red dirty looking set of coaches was stationary and rapidly being filled with eager passengers, hurrying as if their life depended upon it. The conspicuous letters B.R. were clearly printed in gold paint on each of these coaches which distinguished them, being fairly new, from the other trains. The misty windows looked as if they had never been in contact with soap and water but maybe the window cleaner had been too busy. The overworked wheels were excessively sweating oil and vapour after burning up hundreds of miles.

The engine about to pull these coaches looked like a dirty, mechanical monster blowing its top but this did not worry the two confident drivers who just patted it and smiled as if it had been one of their own children or their favourite pet. They knew how to calm it down and make this monstrosity obey their command. As water vapour hissed from the top funnel the engine began to chunt lazily along the gleaming lines and slowly gathered speed until it had been completely devoured by a dark tunnel.

Girl age 13.

Winter Colours

Snow is a thick white blanket
Covering the dull, grey ground
The holly berries are like miniature apples
Ripe and shining red
Christmas decorations are as coloured as autumn leaves
People wear thick, grey clothes
Like a sheep's coat of wool.
These are the winter colours which I think of most.

Girl age 14.

Spring

Spring! excitement, surprise and colour! Spring!
A season of life, a most enjoyable thing.

Winter past, bad weather cast.
She's here, Spring's come at last!

She skates over the beds, dead and brown
Wearing majestic garb and a windy crown.

She draws each snow drop from earth's clutch,
With her strong, steady, magnetic touch.

Daffodil, crocus, hyacinth blue.
A touch of green, such a refreshing hue.

New colours, new songs, a new air too!
Even the sky's a different blue!

Birds chant their songs
That all winter long,
Quelled in their throats
Waiting to break through.

Girl age 14.

Spring

Spring is here,
Winter has fled!
She has awakened the birds
Who sing in the green-specked trees.
Each blade of grass blows
In the fresh Spring breeze.
The tiny coltsfoot throws
Open her lone yellow head
To greet the Spring.
On the beech-tree
Tiny cigar-like buds can be seen.
The leaves on the hawthorn open
After a long winter's dream.

Spring is here,
Winter has fled.
The snowdrop hangs her head
A delicate maid in a green edged toga.
Trumpets of golden daffodils
Sound their fanfare to the Spring
As she flows gently past.
The lambs bleat in the fields.
The radiant blue sky leaves
No trace of winter
Fleecy, white clouds float
Like fluffy mounds of sheared wool.

Girl age 13.

November

November is a month of moods,
Now bright, now dull,
And in the woods
The trees in swan song colours
Stand; but there is no distance.

No distant fields
Or woods, but the chestnut tree
Which opens its spiky case
To reveal its warm-brown nuts
We are always pleased to see.

The hedgerows glisten with tiny drops of clear dew,
The sodden paths are muddy, and the new
White frost is crisp, and yet
Who cares if it's cold and wet!

Girl age 12.

The Witch

Deep in a cave I see
A witch dancing with glee,
Long finger nails, pointed hat,
Broomstick in corner near the cat.
She dances round the huge black pot,
She keeps the fire very hot.
As she dances here, she sings . . .
. . . "In I throw a blackbird's wings,
In goes liver of a frog
In goes rotted wood of a mossy log,
I throw in black cat's eyes
I make this for a man that dies.
Here I throw blood of snakes
And here I put dead fish from lakes.
Bubble, gurgle sings my pot
Must make sure the fire is hot.
Now I throw in finger nails.
Then in go savage starved dogs' tails.
Tomorrow I shall meet this man
And make him drink this if I can.

Alas my feet are feeling cold
Now to say my word so bold
The magic word here I say
Boil, boil, urgle trumpah yay.
Now my evil work is done
I'll ride the sky till the rising moon.

Girl age 13.

Spring

Why does she not sound herself on drums,
Beating a tattoo that she comes,
But no, she peeps coyly round on the barren scene
Then steps out more boldly,
Her yellow attire floating behind her,
For she is Spring, the fairest of them all.

She goes through the beechwoods,
Along frost bitten paths,
Turning even a hard stone
Into a glowing mellowness,
The rested sap rushes involuntarily back to life,
Spiky green shots have pierced earth's shield.

Frail snowdrops delicately formed
Are at first the sole flowers to respond to her touch,
She peeps under hedgerows, and leaves the message behind
For colourful flowers spring to life.
The grey dull stream becomes crystal clear,
Bubbling its mirth over fresh mossy stones.

The bird in the clear blue sky,
Flies in the wind tossing back his throbbing notes.
He preens his feathers, flutters his wings
Then off over the wall he goes,
For he must show his prime to some young girl.
The sun is shining,
But she casts a shower of silver rain
To hurry a few lazy sparks of life along
For she says,
"We must not be late to gladden the hearts
Of the Winter weary mortals".

Girl age 13.

November

A dark leaden sky hung low o'er the town,
No sun glaring down on a dull Autumn day,
No trees with bright coloured leaves,
No birds chanting in the trees,
No flowers blooming in the garden,
Only bare patches of soil, wet in places
And short, silver trails left by the snail,
No bright green grass,
Only wet, soggy ditches.

Work from a country Modern school of about 400 boys and girls streamed according to ability. The school draws from 9 County Primary schools of which the largest is about 200 strong and the smallest 40. The fathers of most of the children work on the land or in the mill. Most of the villages from which the children come have a weaving shed.

If the child is to write freely and willingly then we must ensure that his experience of life and the general cultural conditions of his school are as rich and varied as we can possibly make them. We must try to give to the children we teach what De Selincourt calls

". . . a veritable transcript of life itself."

If the child's experience is a rich one, then he is better equipped to write "freely and willingly" since his interest in the past has been stimulated and he reacts to his work with increased zeal. He must be given opportunity to write and to think, and limits should not be set on time or length of work done. He must sometimes be given choice of subject and always freedom to tackle it in the way he wishes. He must at all times be given encouragement and criticism, not only by the teacher and head teacher but also by his fellow pupils; indeed, I feel that the critical suggestions of fellow pupils often produce a vigorous improvement in the quality of work done. He must constantly be stimulated with varied examples of literature chosen by the teacher. He must be ready to read his work aloud to the class and comment upon it. Most important perhaps and springing from the successful application of these criteria, he must develop a sincerity and justifiable pride in his work.

Generally in this school work is corrected promptly, the following procedure being current. "S" in the margin denotes a spelling mistake, "P" denotes punctuation and "E" (English) denotes mistakes of usage and expression. With classes of low ability the more obvious mistakes only are corrected and it is felt that an encouraging remark by the teacher is of more value than a welter of red correction signs. Corrections are not done after every piece of written work but are entered periodically into a small English notebook in the correct form — once — and learnt.

We try to teach spelling in a preventive rather than a curative way. Every child has a dictionary which he is encouraged to use in every lesson and from time to time lists of words are given to the children to learn, the emphasis here being on accuracy and brevity and not on tedious repetition. When it is felt that a point of punctuation or usage can with value be explained to and practised with the class then this is done by the whole class, but generally it is felt that more is achieved by personal discussion of individual errors between the pupil and the teacher.

Little, if any, use is made of text books containing so-called "graded exercises". These books have for long been anathema to me.

Boy age 11.

The Fox

Sleek, sly and sharp,
The fox is on the run,
The hens are wary,
The moonlight strong,
The fox is on the run,
The hens shivering,
The dogs trembling,
It is midnight,
The fox is getting nearer,
It prowls around the hen hut,
It creeps through the entrance,
Then a scream, squawk and shuffle,
Then all goes quiet,
The fox comes out
With a hen in its mouth,
An then goes off in the dark to devour its prey.

Girl age 12.

The Playground

Boys fighting,
Girls playing ball,
Boys play at hopscotch,
But the knitting of the girls goes on.
Boys play cricket,
Girls talking to boys,
Boys shouting and yelling,
But the knitting of the girls goes on.
Boys and girls come out from dinner,
Girls and boys doing long jump,
Girls sunbathing on the field,
Boys trying to show off,
But the knitting of the girls goes on.
They hear the bell,
And the knitting of the girls stops.

Girl age 13.

In the Evening

Picks and shovels put aside,
Boots are polished with skill and care,
As one by one the navvy men set out to enjoy themselves.
Six full days of working, sweat, toil and misery.
And what do you get to repay your toil?
A grubby pay packet!
But at least it's good and honest work,
And it keeps the hungry mouths of your family shut.

The contrast to the cold night air
In the small and grimy pub,
The hazy smoke, the drink and sweat,
Is alarmingly different, when you come to think.
A small boy blinks uncertainly,
His first time in a pub.
He glances at the bar-maid,
A friendly-looking woman, powdered and blushing,
At the rough-voiced compliments.

"What'll you have?" comes a boisterous voice
From a small squat man,
The landlord, a sly, bowlegged man,
A gentleman of his class, grins easily,
But the nervous lad takes to his heels
And bolts.

Girl age 13.

A Wild Bird

It stood in all its glory, bedraggled and conceited. Its
neck so naked, its face so ugly, its claws like giant's feet.
That beak was pointed, long, sharp and narrow to peck the
flesh of man bird and beast. Its eyes looked evil, wicked
and treacherous.

The vulture the bird of prey.

Boy age 13.

Ghosts

The dark sky,
The full moon,
A short cut through the graveyard,
A low cloud comes rolling in,
It shrinks into a ball,
Then parts extended
To look like a man.

They turned and ran,
Eyes in bushes,
Eyes on nowhere,
Smoke, devils' smoke,
Dead men rise,
The sign of death.
Then, a flash in the sky,
Rain, they don't like rain,
They disappear,
And you are safe,
For now.

Boy age 13.

A Hot Day

One day when the bell rang for play time we all ran out onto the playfield. Because it was so hot most of us lay down to keep cool. I was lying down half-asleep thinking of the swimming pool which the school intend to build on the field. I was thinking of the way we could build it ourselves if we each took a spade and volunteered to dig it in our own spare time. I was still thinking of the hours of enjoyment the swimming pool would give us.

Suddenly the bell went and startled me. When I got into the suffocating class-room the teacher said, "Who would like to go on the field and work?" All the hands went up and so we went onto the field for the lesson. Some of us only half worked and I was one of them. I was busy watching the farmer I often help. He was haymaking in the next field and I could see Maurice baling the hay by forking the hay from pikes and ricks. Faintly but being able to tell what the sound was I could hear the click of the knot-maker tieing knots in the string round the bales before they would come out of the machine. Then I was called to attention and worked till the bell went and we were released at last.

Boy age 13.

Aftermath

The fair was over and the strenuous job of packing up had begun. The men set to work vigorously, down came the stalls and into the wagons they were packed. The swing-boats were dismantled and packed away. Then the "dodgems" were pulled down and put into wagons. All the litter had been picked up and the refuse wagon had come to collect it. The wagon lurched suddenly and skidded as it tried to leave the field, at last it managed to churn its way out of the field. A last minute check to see that everything was in order and then the wagons pulled out one by one, skidding as they moved slowly through the deep mud which clung to the tyres. They spun helplessly as if in an attempt to free themselves from its grip. At last the wagons were on the road and on their way to the next town.

The field lay silent, everywhere was mud. Near the gateway were deep ruts full of water. Great muddy puddles lay everywhere. The grass was yellow where the vehicles and stalls had stood. Soddened straw lay everywhere. Footprints of many different sizes dotted the squalid ground. The smell of soddened grass filled the air.

The rain poured down again, filling every vacant hole and rut and making the field like a bog. The wind ruffled the grass and snatched the litter, lifting it high in the air and then letting it fall to the ground. The fair was over and the fun had finished for that year.

Girl age 13.

From the Mill

Every night at five-thirty the mill buzzer goes and all the people stop work. Then they all rush out to catch their buses and trains. The workers are men and women, young and old; most of them are dressed in shabby clothes. Men in overalls and dirty raincoats, women in old coats and pinafores.

Mary D ... is one of the many women amongst them. She has to work hard to keep her family and her husband who is unemployed. She knows that her three children will be waiting for her when she gets home. Down the street she rushed just in time to catch her bus. When she got home she found her two youngest children in bed with 'Flu. She went to the house next door to see if she could use the 'phone to call the doctor. When she got back home it was half-past six and her husband was wanting his tea.

"Where have you been?" he asked.

"I only went next door," she replied.

"I want my tea!" he demanded.

After tea when the pots had been washed Mary took her vacuum cleaner and began to sweep the carpet.

"Must you do that?" said her husband.

"Yes," said Mary, "You know the doctor is coming tomorrow so the house must be cleaned."

At half-past seven Mary said to her husband, "Take the dog for a walk, dear."

'Why should I always take the dog out?" he said.

"It was you who wanted the dog to help you to catch rabbits," she retorted.

Girl age 14.

My Earliest Recollections

It was mid-summer and the days were hot and long. Alongside of my friend's house was a small, cool stream. We were in our first weeks at school and shrimps had been a topic that day. So we decided we should go shrimping that day.

It was a lovely stream, it gurgled and sprang along, twisting and turning along its rocky path. The stream came from the ground and beside the beginning of the stream was a large stone well, covered in curtains of green moss and other species. The well overflowed frequently and this, added to the extent of the spouting water from the ground, made a small pond. All this seemed to assure us that shrimps must exist in this water. So, aided with sea-side buckets, spades, a sieve and several other valuable pieces of equipment, we set off on our "shrimping expedition". We wallowed in the mud for hours till it was dusk. Tired, wet and weary we went home disappointed and demanding of our parents why shrimps did not live in our pool.

Besides these various exploits I always — this is before starting school and up to the age of eight, played with the boys, there being no more girls to play with and having a brother of my own. During the summer we played cricket on the lawn in front of our houses. The boys, being quite a bit older than myself, manhandled the full size cricket bat with ease, but I had to heave it from wicket to wicket, till in desperation they would send me home.

While in summer we played cricket, so in winter we started our football season. This, by far, was my favourite pastime. We charged about the street kicking, screaming at one another, and on numerous occasions the ball landed in neighbouring gardens and, being the smallest I was pushed through the hedge, my small jeans caught and tore at the pricking hedge. When I returned, having retrieved the football, I was a hero and was heartily slapped on the back and was told I could go again if I wanted. Sometimes they got thoroughly sick of me. Once, I remember, they said I could be the Indian and they tied me to someone's clothes pole and left me till dinner-time.

Trainspotting was also one of my pastimes. We would soar up the tree in the goodsyard and sit for hours on end waiting and waiting. Once, through the excitement of seeing a big express and the vibration, I went headlong into the clump of nettles below.

We had occasional visits from a friend up the road, whom we were not very fond of. One day we took him prisoner and tied him head and foot, a bucket on his head and a banana skin in his mouth. I do not think his mother was very pleased about the situation.

They emigrated to Australia several months later.

Boy age 14.

The Scar

Three hundred feet and more
It rises high, its summit in the clouds,
Grey and unmolested,
It leans, solitary and unrivalled.

Only the isolated and lonely bird
Soars around its desolate pinnacle,
Occasionally landing on a slimy ledge
And uttering its harsh cry.

It stands,
Centuries old,
Looking on the green patchwork quilt below.

A mixed Grammar school of 829 pupils serving a mainly rural area.

We believe that regular practice is the key to progress in the effective writing of English. Children must begin young and write regularly. Adequate time must be spent on the preparation, writing, reading and assessment of compositions.

To follow up to compositions is most important. When the compositions have been completed, half a dozen are read to the class by the writers and the children are encouraged to make reasoned comments on matter, style and arrangement. These comments, together with the teacher's own assessment, give the children a greater awareness of levels of expression than a general comment from the teacher could ever do. Children begin to know what is expected and what is possible.

A great deal of importance is attached to reading as an aid to writing. Children are actively encouraged to develop the reading habit. They are urged to use the School Libraries, County Libraries and to develop Form Libraries (mainly good paperbacks). Wide and selective reading gives the child an appreciation of style and is a painless way of acquiring an expressive vocabulary. Books read in literature periods are carefully chosen and an attempt is made to make the study of literature an enjoyable experience. Even at an early stage close study is made of particularly good passages of prose and verse. These elementary exercises in criticism are designed to develop a feeling for language.

The paragraph is found to be a convenient unit for developing habits of effective expression. A paragraph on a limited topic is written, read, assessed and revised in the space of a single English period. Single sentences are sometimes written. These are based on a simple idea and the results subjected to detailed critical evaluation by the class.

Pupils who read and write regularly seem to need little formal instruction in English Grammar (or spelling and punctuation for that matter!). We use no set grammar text book in this school. Grammar is administered in small digestible doses and pupils gradually compile their own notebooks. To further the aim of relating the various aspects of English teaching we study the workings of grammar "live" in the books being studied in Literature.

We have a prose and verse competition with external assessors and the more promising work is published in the School Magazine. A Special English Prize open to all pupils, with a junior and senior section, is also presented on the basis of reviews of novels, poems, etc., a reading and an interview with English staff and interested governors of the school.

A lively and sensitive approach is perhaps the most important single factor. If the teacher can communicate his own enthusiasm this will go a long way towards stimulating an interest in writing. If children enjoy their English, both reading and writing, real progress can be made.

Girl age 13.
Form 3A.

Refugees

Dragging feet, slurring along an unknown road,
Dull eyes deadened by life-long fear,
Blank faces, suspiciously regarding authority,
For authority killed their loved ones;
Drove them from their homes to wander in a foreign land,
To shelter in cardboard shacks provided by some friendly
    organisation.

Trudging desolately away,
Leaving all they know,
Clutching their few possessions
Pathetically bundled together.
Children squalling, frightened.
Families fleeing, with their lives
Held in the hands of warriors.
Here are the sufferers from the senseless wars,
The remainders of war's destruction, the ones who are
    perpetual reminders
Of all that man creates in order to destroy.
The hopeless ones — the refugees.

Girl age 14.
Form 4JS.

As the sun rose so would Irish Peter. At the crack of dawn he would bathe in the nearby stream, after first carefully putting his paper blankets away.

At the end of the summer, as the world seemed to be preparing for sleep, we would see less and less of old Peter.

Years would come and go but no-one could find out where he spent the long cold winters.

Everyone, especially the very young, adored Irish Peter. His long hair curling at his collar, the red beard of Santa Claus in his youth, even the white shirt that not even a detergent could get so sparkling. The mischievous boys would try to torment him, but they knew that they could never win, Irish Peter had no bad temper, he took everything in his stride.

Girl age 14.
Form 4GL.

A Pencil

As I write a pencil lies before me, and as I look at it, I want to give a description of it to you, the reader.

The pencil is long, slim, and elegant, with a hexagonal cross section. At one end it has been cut away to form a point, but it has not been cut smoothly, as it would have been by a pencil sharpener. No, it is rather rough, with ridges and valleys in the shaven wood. The point of graphite and clay, which we ignorantly call lead, is not smooth, but has a jagged, triangular cross-section. The other end, still untouched, I am glad to say, has a slightly convex end-covering of black paint. This paint passes down the side of the pencil for about one thirtysecond of an inch, where it is bordered by a beautiful contrasting section of pure white. This is not very thick, however, and the rest of the pencil is painted a rich red on five of its flat faces, broken only by five thin straight bands of black, passing right down to the cut away end.

The sixth face is different, however; it is black. Two parallelograms of gold, one at one end, one at the centre of this black face, bear the bold letters: H.B. The rest of this black face is only broken by the lettering in proud gold: 200 C J S Staedtler Tradition GERMANY. About two inches away from the point end lie two marks which are the only ones spoiling its smooth beauty. They are about one half of an inch apart and are in the form of arcs of a circle, scars left by a compass, and scars which it will carry for the rest of its life.

Girl age 14.
Form 4KB.

Murder

Chapter One

Towards dusk, one misty November evening, a shabby, five ton lorry with its three passengers slowly made its way down the narrow stony lane, half hidden between over-hanging bushes. It was an eerie place, little used by the public, and appeared to lead nowhere. The day had been long and dreary, and the collection of scrapmetal none too profitable so far, and tempers were more than a little frayed.

Clogger, the gauky youth, was all for "packing it in"; he was cold, tired, and his stomache felt empty. Besides the other two men he looked like a schoolboy, with his thin bony wrists protruding beyond the ends of his frayed jacket, which hung off his thin narrow shoulders. He had sharp features, very pallid, and his open mouth revealed an array of discoloured, irregular teeth. His hair drooped limply over his forehead and hung in a fringe over the back of his worn collar . . .

His uncle Mick shut him up roughly, and thought that they might have a bit more luck with this their last call. Mick was a powerfully built man, perhaps even bigger than Josh, and he had an uncertain temper; it was better to keep on the right side of him. More than once he had been on the wrong side of the law.

The driver and owner of the lorry, Josh, merely grunted and kept his eyes on the road. He was not one for arguments; action was more in his line . . . How he and Mick had joined up was something of a mystery, but they were thought of as a couple of shady characters who perhaps knew too much about each other.

H

Chapter Two

At length the lorry turned slowly and cautiously onto a small patch of waste ground at the end of the lane, and the noisy engine ground to a halt. It sounded quiet in the cab and was rather cosy and warm from the heat of the engine. Clogger felt drowsy and wished he hadn't to get out into the raw air, but his uncle's huge fist between his shoulders soon persuaded him.

The old scrap dealer who had the reputation of "having a bit put by" was nowhere in sight. He lived — perhaps "existed" would be a better word — in a low stone shed with a sloping slate roof, through which a battered stove-pipe pushed its way. From it came a thin wisp of smoke, and Clogger eyed it hopefully. The only source of light appeared to be a tiny window let in one side, but even this was almost hidden by a ragged elderberry bush . . .

Girl age 14.
Form 4A.

A Hillside in the Sun

A golden flower beneath a golden skirt
And sun on a white and dappled house, with trees;
A brook in living browny shade mutters among its tawny
    stones.
Sun, sun, everywhere; the grass caressed by the constant
    sleepy summer-gold sun.
Smoke blue-drifting, curling, up to the gentian sky,
Where the sun beats upon the six of us, drawing, sleeping,
    quiet, still.
No sound but the sound of a bird and a brook;
And there, in the sun-coloured streets, hums a motor-bike.
Pools of gold, of amber shade, of rainbow-dryad water
Gurgle in wonder at their warmth.
Soak up the sun like honey, sweet, mellow, embracing
Drown in the heat that laps the edges of your mind
And melts so softly, slowly into the paling gold beyond
And sleep . . . is there.

Girl age 15.
Form 5HH.

At the Hairdresser's

Fritz, or Fred to his assistants, minced up and down the salon in his white bootees, smoking an expensive "Black Russian" cigarette and waving a pair of slender scissors. Everything in the salon was shrouded in pink. It was like a sort of pink fungus growing everwhere. A balmy, slightly sickening smell penetrated every corner of the salon.

The only things that spoiled the pink scenery were the rusty dirty bins underneath the sinks, revealed only when the assistants whisked aside the pink frilly curtains to hastily push in some shorn locks of hair, then, even more quickly, whisked them back again. A brown crack in the bowl of the sink was the only visible flaw in Fritz's little pink world.

A plump, middle-aged lady was sitting underneath a humming hair-dryer, nervously flicking over the pages of a glossy fashion magazine. As I watched, her round face seemed to be getting redder and redder. She was vainly trying to shrink down into the pink foam-cushioned chair, but her plumpness hindered her. I suddenly realised that the hair-dryer was burning her. All the assistants wandered past her, quite oblivious of her plight. Unable to stand it any longer, I jumped up and hurried over to the woman, who was now a decided purple in colour. Quickly I switched the control down to "cool" and after receiving a grateful smile from the lady, who was now returning to a natural pink colour, I returned to my seat.

Fritz, who was to cut my hair, advanced, brandishing a razor. He smiled, revealing two dark grey fillings on his bottom row of teeth. I wondered that they too were not pink. He spoke to me with an accentuated foreign accent. He was just about to start slicing through my mass of hair when an ear-splitting scream vibrated around the salon. Fritz dashed out of my cubicle and into the adjacent one. It seemed that a rather flashy woman of about fifty, who changed the colour of her hair as regularly as her bedclothes, had asked for a platinum blonde rinse and it had turned out a brassy yellow.

Fritz, after unsuccessfully trying defensive tactics, switched to the offensive and started shouting. Half way through his ravings, he dropped his polished foreign accent and shouted out in "broad Yorkshire". A few minutes later, she stormed out of the salon, threatening to sue Fritz for every penny he had!

Fritz, erupting with anger, returned to my cubicle and started hacking at my hair. I watched as he vented his wrath on my poor defenceless locks.

Boy age 16.
Form 6 Modern.

The Salmon

Full of hope, full of life, she has come from the heaving Atlantic, and now in the dark calm of the estuary she rests, with the dull boom of the retching ocean still sounding from beyond the bluff. She rests, amassing within her that force which has lain quiescent all the late summer, and now is stirred by Nature into a consuming fire.

Suddenly the effervescent spark burns white-hot and with a twist she is gone, flicking through the shore pools of mottled light towards her destined spawning ground.

She leaps glistening over the boiling cataracts and rises dripping into the sunlight — a mere flash of the silver-white belly and the dull shine of the gun-metal head — and then she drops again into the water above the falls to continue her relentless journey up the river's autumnal flood.

Night and day this goes on until she reaches that familiar rocky pool of green pebbly shadow, secluded in a wooded glen,— that same pool she visited last autumn, and the one before . . . and the one before that . . .

But for the first time the leafy solitude of this pool is ruffled. The exhausted salmon catches sight of something dancing in the sun just below the surface, something more beautiful than anything she has ever seen. The moving creature tantalises the fish, and lured on by its gaudy colours and fluted shape quivering in the shallows, the salmon darts nearer and swerves by, leaving the prize swaying delicately in a stream of bubbles. Once more she circles and then with one lunge gulps the treasure down.

In a second the angler tears the hook from the salmon's throat, and stuffing the fish in his bag, makes his way back home.

Boy age 17.
Form 6² Science.

Tragedy in Trilogy

Pre-flight

The tower of steel tracery rumbles back.
A slender steel pencil points to the sky.

A slight breeze raises tiny clouds of dust,
Whistles through the coarse grass of the Florida dunes
And carries a plume of vapour out to the distant shore
Where the sea pounds the deserted beach.

The sky above has the cold grey face of dawn
Where, even yet, the last stars of night twinkle undimmed.
But slowly the sun will rise,
Its first rays will strike the tip of this thin sliver of steel
And creeping down it show the frosted sides.

For here, scarcely a few hours past
Under the glare of arc lights
The last liquid oxygen was pumped on board.
Now, icy cold, the extra gas seeps out,
And floats, a plume of vapour, out to sea.

The sun is risen, the sky is blue,
The sand shines gold and the surf gleams white.
The rocket has a silver sheen
A silver pencil waits to write across the sky.

Boy aged 17.
Form 6² Science.

Song of a Commercial

I'm a commercial, I am.
Yes, I am a commercial, I am.
I jingle and jangle,
My words are a tangle,
I'm only there to confuse.

Washing machines, spin driers as well,
Tobacco, I am just burning to sell.
With that family scene, or those rivers and trees,
I can sell anything, all that you please.

The praises I sing, both loud and long
Of soap demonstrations that never go wrong
I'm musical too, my own trumpet I blow,
I play high and loud, then soft and low.

Boy age 17.
Form 6² Science.

Post-mortem

With an air of morbid gloom
Engineers gather in the conference room
And, with a bored familiarity,
Strive to come to parity,
To rise like Phoenix from the ashes,
The cold ashes of defeat.

To give excuses and white lies,
Why their bird fell from the skies
The story they tell is ever the same
Each on others will place the blame.

Telemetry blames the fuel,
The Chemist would toll the motor's knell
While Engineers accuse control.

But the wreckage holds a shock for all;
A short examination settles it —
The blue touch paper never lit.

A Girls' Grammar school of 706 pupils in the Heavy Woollen district.

It is much easier to recognise a successful piece of writing than to explain what makes it so. What qualities in a piece of prose or verse make us say: "This is good. This achieves what the writer meant to achieve"? Freshness, vitality, authenticity and unity of tone, individual choice of word and phrase, these at any rate are among the things we look for.

First of all the children need to be launched, to be given an impetus and started on their way. The most obvious means of doing this is to give them a choice of interesting subjects on which to write, and this often works well. They may be started off by listening to an interesting piece of someone else's writing — a description of white tiger cubs from The Times, *D. H. Lawrence's account of the behaviour of a wild rabbit, "Adolf" or James Kirkup's sensations underground in the Mendip hills. Good writing sometimes follows interesting conversation in class; for example, about grandparents, 'bus conductors or television personalities.*

Next, it is essential for the teacher to give full and serious attention to whatever work is produced, to comment on it in detail and to praise anything he possibly can in the ideas or the expression. Destructive criticism rarely does any good and it may paralyse completely, whereas encouragement works wonders.

Some of the prose writing done will be of considerable length: plays in several acts, "novels" and autobiographies running perhaps to ten or twenty chapters. This sustained effort of writing over a number of weeks is highly educative, but it is, by its very nature, difficult to give examples of.

Free verse is a particularly useful medium for self expression. It often brings a sense of release to the writer just because it is not ordinary, workaday prose. Unusual words and turns of phrase can be introduced into it without their sounding unnatural. It can sweep aside many of the inhibitions which hold up free expression in prose. It has advantages too over more formal types of verse because it avoids that desperate search for the rhyming word and the line which contains a set number of syllables.

There must be a feeling of confidence and relaxation in the group if good work is to be done. The pupil needs to feel that what she writes will be attended to sympathetically. But no recipe for success can be given. Sometimes the most carefully planned efforts end in failure. Sometimes good writing is sparked off at the most unexpected moment but whenever and wherever it comes one accepts it gratefully.

Girl age 11.

My Dog

There was a little dog,
That was my little dog,
I took him out every day,
I loved him in a special way.

Girl age 12.

A Strange Visitor

I was standing alone in the silent church, after a service. All was still. There was no movement except the occasional scratching of the rats and mice behind the panels. The parson had gone, the organist had gone, and all the congregation had gone. I was all alone in a dim, dusty, ghostly place. If you have ever been in as silent a place as this, with no one but the rats and mice to keep you company, you will know how horrible and lonely it feels. I felt as though I wanted to run away from that still place for ever, but my feet stayed in the same place, facing the organ. Suddenly the organ struck a few notes, yet there was no one there. I was terrified. There was a dim mist around the organ, and the church had a dank smell all around it. The mist began to clear. As it cleared it revealed a young woman with a pale face, sitting at the organ. I recognised her as Amy B . . ., the young girl of the big house who had died five years before of a certain fever whose dread symptoms were still rife throughout the village. I turned to run, but a thought made me turn back. If this was Amy B . . . in a ghostly form, she might speak to me. Suddenly it seemed as if she realised for the first time that there was someone else in the church besides her. She turned. As she did so the moonlight caught her face. It was a face that looked so sad and lonely that I was suddenly quite sorry for her. Then she spoke.

"I know you," she said in a funny voice. "You are Annis B . . ., that girl at the cottage next to the little shop on the corner."

"Yes," I answered, "I am."

She continued, "Those magnolias, are they real?"

"They are real," I said, as I followed her shaking finger to the flowers on the altar.

"Fetch them here," she said in a faint, almost dead voice. I did.

"Put them round my grave." I did this also.

"Now," she said, "take this." "This" was a dagger, brought out from under her cloak. She then got into her grave and lay still in the coffin.

"Kill me," she said slowly. I was shocked.

"Kill you," I echoed.

"Yes, kill me," she said impatiently.

"Yes," I said meekly, and covering my eyes with my arm, I struck as hard and as near to the heart as I could. She sighed and kicked as though still alive, then she was dead. Just then the parson came running in. "I heard you talk-" he said, then stopped dead as he saw the body lying in the grave, uncovered.

"I-I-er think we had better cover her," I said.

"Yes," said the parson, "I think we had." We then lifted the cover and between us got it back over the body.

"A rather strange visitor, don't you think?"

"Yes," said the parson, "I think she was."

Girl age 12.

Fog

How strange the world looks
Under the blanket of oblivion!
The trees appear distorted maniacs
Arrested while flailing their stupid limbs insanely.
Fog —
The very word
Gropes and fumbles
As if confused by its own irony.

Looming to reeling heights beyond the sky,
Houses are ships that pass in the peculiar night,
Giving no clues to their identity.
            How loud my footsteps sound!
How they boom!
I am the only person left on earth;
This is my kingdom,
Confused and silent,
And its king is blind as a bat.

Girl age 13.

In summer the path is at its most friendly. I resent its
cheerful presence, for I come to think and to ponder on
life, completely alienated. I resent the cheerful couples on
the dusty-coloured seats. They are oblivious to me, but I
am all too aware of them. Seldom do I walk there in
complete happiness; if I do, the soft, wiry green grass
and tiny yellow cinquefoil flowers, and the insolent purple
weeds are pleasing to me in the sunlight; usually I prefer
it in the summer rain showers. Then the grass is fresh as
in Spring. The mud and small rain pools remind me of the
pink blossoms which I saw scattered by wind and rain
only a few weeks before. Now they are gone.

I still think of this day when I walk through mud and
drizzle, but at the moment it seems an impossible figment
of my imagination.

The young trees hold up their arms, pitifully, to the sky,
trying to stretch out their snow covered roots. All things
are either black or white. Only the soft pink of the afternoon
sun takes away the harshness. There is no visible life,
everything is stiff, bright and dead.

Yet I enjoy this atmosphere unthinkingly. I think
deeply, with nothing to distract me, nothing to cross the
wandering paths of my mind. From this sanctuary I always
return refreshed and calm.

Girl age 13.

Windfall Apples

In the orchard in the morn,
Upon the dewy ground,
Many little apples red,
Sweet and good I found.

I picked them up so carefully,
And put them in a box.
I polished them to rosy red;
They shone like silky locks.

I thought how wonderful they looked
So smooth and good and round,
We do nothing to deserve them,
We just find them on the ground.

Girl age 13.

A Siamese Cat

I have a Siamese cat who is very beautiful like all his breed, with extreme intelligence and a great sense of humour. Often he will sit on the floor, and watch my baby sister endeavouring to stand, and all the time there is an understanding smile on his face. He will sit on the table while I am struggling with some difficult algebraical problem and insist on washing out my ears, purring loudly in between licks. As you can imagine, it is very distracting. At other times he will sit forlornly on the floor by the cellar door, wailing miserably at everybody who passes by, waiting for his tea.

When it is raining, and he wants to go out, he sits on the doorstep, outstretched, his very wet, very cold, and very shiny nose delicately twitching in the damp air. If then he eventually decides it is worth taking a risk, he elegantly lifts a silken brown paw, and places the soft pads down on the edge of a puddle, then withdraws disdainfully, and shakes the paw with a look of disgust upon his face.

In the wind, which he hates, he puts his ears back as far as they will go and shrinks away from it, snaking his head from side to side, trying to find a patch of calm air.

When it is his meal time he will sit on the kitchen table, his lustrous sapphire eyes watching every movement of your hands, his black tail twitching slightly at the kinked tip. If he is purring upon your lap, and he suddenly smells kippers, his neck becomes twice its original size, his ears flick irritatedly and the whole of his body becomes tense and taut with eagerness, whilst once more his tail twitches in anxiety and anticipation.

It is practically impossible to describe what my dear cat is like in character and looks, but I shall always remember his very fat tummy, his ebony black tail, his tiny brown velveteen paws, his eager eyes and shiny, black, ice-cold nose.

Girl age 14.

The Tree

I see a tree, light, shade, motion, in pale green shooty bloom; gnarled twisted fingersome branches, pale, quivering clusterings of shelving leaves casting grey-blue shadow on the grass beneath, clumps of springy, prickly turf.

The tree is green predominant, supreme, standing under the pale blue of heaven, under the fluorescent, gelatinous sky, cotton-boll'd and whiting, sharp, stark, flat, its dampening leaves of yellow and jewelled green; stunted, austere, and sturdy, peopled by a speckled throstle and her elastic-jawed young, in downy, fluffy young feathers of white.

A hawk is circling; a coal-black dot, in an azure, foaming sky. He falls, and snatches at his defenceless prey. A scream, a flutter of feathers, in the heavy, oppressive air. All is silence. The hawk is hungry no more, nor are his babes, but the throstle fledgelings will be hungry unto death.

The mate flutters spasmodically in disappointed, baffled grief, and then falls, a broken stone. His life is gone, he is dead.

The hawk, with one last triumphant wheel, the broken neck and drooping, bleeding head of the speckled throstle swinging to and fro from his curved, slicing jaws, gives one last screech of bloody triumph, one last gasp upon the grave.

Only the live and silent sentinel of pain, free from awful earthly dry-rot treasures, and sweet triumphant death are left, death, the gate through which we pass, on our way to freedom from out hated earthly gain.

The tree stands guard o'er all the realms of nature past and present. The tree is a perfect thing, glistening, a many-faceted emerald in the shimmering heat of the upper fields.

Girl age 14.

My Brother

He went to the ant, the sluggard,
He squashed it with his foot.
There was nothing left on the hard grey earth
But a little blood.
My brother gave a leering grin,
Then quoth he cheerily,
"Another ant is dead and gone,
Dead with foot,
It is dead and I did it.
With my foot I killed it,
Dead,
Gone;
Poor little ant."
This is an illustration
Of my brother's twisted mind.
We can do nothing but pray for him.
What a pity!
He used to be quite sane,
As sane as all our family,
But now I fear he is gone.
We can do nothing but pray for him.
What a pity!

Girl age 14.

Return to the Moors

The undulating quietness amazed me at first
And in bewilderment I searched for a hill
With an outline strong and comforting,
But there was nothing to take away the ache,
No towering height to awe into nothingness the void
    inside me.
My thoughts and hopes were centred on the scenes I loved
    and missed.
Where were the wild free moors, the gaunt bleakness
Of a beloved birthplace?
The air was soft, warm and peaceful,
Everything was green, fresh and clean,
The ideal setting for a happy, sheltered life;
But much as I enjoyed the soft breezes, they seemed strange
    and foreign,
For deep inside me were the winds of the moors,
Proud, untamed and relentless.
When I eventually returned from the fertile lowlands of
    the South,
I realised how much I had missed the moors, the wind,
    the hills.
Once again, I was able to climb almost to heaven
To lose my fears, doubts and suspicions
In the glorious freedom of the moorland world.

Girl age 16.

Laburnum

In idle sadness
The heavy drops
Pollen-filled
Tremble in the Spring breeze;
A profuseness of pale yellow
Vibrating,
A foil of muted green —
A shower of gold
Upon a slender stem,
O, prophetess of Summer,
O, delicate witch.

Girl age 17.

Leaves of Light and Shade

In twilight's blue a shiver of coolness
Splashes through the air,
And the thick layers of thin leaves
Ripple and lap at the wall's edge.
Shadows pool across the cool stone
And break in liquid darkness,
Flowing, trickling, spreading
Under the dusty glow
Of the spindly, flickering lamp.

These leaves of light and shade
Dry and fade, fall, and billow
Against the well in rushing depths.
Stars shiver their splintered white light
And a smudge of blurred orange-red moon
With furred edges peers through hollow darkness
And sharp, thin, clutching branches.
Delicate skeletons of leaves
Twitch and shudder, and dull clouds
Slither by, furtive, wary.

Girl age 18.

Reflections on Holiday

I sat in the sand dunes, the wind blowing all-pervading particles of sand into my hair, eyes, even my teeth, and surveyed the scene before me. Seagulls were arguing over a mysterious-looking object cast up by the sea, vivid with its shades of green and silver as seen from a distance. Children were playing with heaps of coloured stones, making patterns on the light brown sand. Far out a man was digging for mussels in the soft, dark, sea-wet sand of the bay, strong and capable with his open sack beside him, bending and thrusting against a spade with a foot clad in a large black wellington boot, turning over piles of sand to view the smooth wave pattern left by the sea. Further out still, cargo boats, grey and orange, serviceable, yet with an air of mystery, moved slowly along an invisible river in the centre of the wide expanse of sand, grey trails of smoke just to be seen against the still grey sky, with now and then the sound of a far off hooter, sad and wistful. Other ships passed along the waterway to the sea: merry little tugs hustling the large slow vessels: purposeful trawlers moving to far off fishing grounds, perhaps off the coast of Iceland, seal waters cold and black with gunboats guarding the harvest of the sea, herrings and cod swimming in silvery shoals among the deep waters.

Suddenly the scene changed, the wind dropped; a grey curtain of rain descended between me and the ships: the children disappeared as if by magic, and I was left to make my way back towards the far distant colourful lights of the town along a beach deserted but for a miserable, wet, straggly, long-haired dog, struggling onward against the force of the wind and rain.

Chapter IV

RECENT CHANGES IN THE LEARNING OF ENGLISH IN JUNIOR SCHOOLS

It was stated at the beginning of the last chapter that more examples had been taken from Junior schools because it was in these schools that the greatest progress had been made in recent years.

Although, no doubt, ten years ago an anthology of good work by individual children of Junior school age could have been made, it certainly was not possible then to find whole schools producing work of the kind taken from the ten schools quoted in the preceding chapter.

Although it is true to say that even twenty years ago some Infant schools were moving rapidly towards the production of good personal writing, there were others, as indeed there still are, which confined their pupils to the use of words of one syllable, insisting that these be copied into books before anything more ambitious was attempted. The child's expressions were not allowed to outstrip his ability to spell.

This is by no means an accurate impression of what now happens in many schools. Once children have made any start at all they are encouraged to write as fluently and copiously as their abilities will allow. The following piece is an attempt by a boy of modest ability to record his ambitions. It was written before he was six, at a time when some equally able children are still writing laboriously "Tom got his cap wet".

> *"When I grow up*
> I like to be a barber cose you Get a Rayt Lot of Moniy and in yor shop you Get a Rayt Lot of PePeL in yor ShoP Thay av bayds I will Put bill krim on thar her I like to cut mashtashase Sum men will brinG ther little boys to av ther little boys her kut I like to Put sheyvinsowP on ther

fayses and sheyv it off I want to be a barber naw I will
Giv them shotbackandsayd kruwcot sqerneck I seL
rasabLads shavin Loshan shavinsowP and biLcriym I
shaL chath the Men 3 shiLig and boLd men 2 shiLig and
boys 6 Pans."

Two years later he was writing with equal fluency, but much
greater accuracy, thus —

"Mrs perkins put on her hat and picked her big basket
up and went to the village and she boght some extra
strong medicine she bought some meat, bread, potatoes,
cabbage, onions, carrots, milk, tea, coffee, sugar, cream,
suit, flour, eggs, jam, treakle and strawberries. Mr. Perkins
had a dose of the medicine. Mrs Perkins cooked a lovely
dinner and it smelt so delicous that he felt quite hungry
so he asked if he could come down in his dressing gown
and they all shouted Hurrah the next morning there was
terrific rattatat it was the postman and he had two fat
envelopes . . ."

At the Junior stage the change has been different. Some years ago
it was customary for the teacher carefully to prescribe, or at least to
circumscribe, what the child wrote, so that what was eventually
produced was in the teacher's eyes appropriate in matter, style and
degree of difficulty.

In the late forties in a Junior school directed by an experienced
Headmaster the ablest child wrote this piece, which bears the stamp
of what the teacher believed to be the sort of thing that a nice little
girl of ten ought to write —

"*The Canary*
I am a yellow canary and I live in a beautiful cage of
gold. I know that I should be happy, but I'm not. My
little misstress and master hang me up at the window.
After my breakfast, and at dinner-time I am lifted down.
After dinner I have a nap, and wake up in time for tea.

The little pink cloth which every canary should have is put over my cage at eight o'clock at night, and taken away at eight o'clock in the mornig. Some-times, for a treat, my mistress comes and talks to me before bedtime, so I sing her a special song. With all these things I should be happy, but I would rather be flying free outside."

The Headmaster changed his views on teaching some years after this was written and almost everything in his school changed. The kind of English now produced is illustrated by the following two pieces by children of the same age but much less able than the one who wrote about the canary.

"My Dad

My dad seems to be a gentle sort of bloke at first glance, but when he is in a mad rage he looks like the devil himself. His head goes red and then he goes a deep purple and HELL goes up. His belt comes off and he looks like a rogue elephant on the rampage. He picks up a chair and threatens to throw it at us. When his temper eases up a bit he sits himself down in a chair exhausted. Still my dad's not a bad chap and he's always one for a joke. My dad's rather like my grandad, always in bed and fagged out when he comes from the pit. My dad goes a bit eccentric when the wireless is on, he dances about like Gina Lolobrigida in pit boots."

"Bolton and its Surroundings

The school stands out against other houses and buildings because it is surrounded by green lawns and a large field. Groups of semi-detached houses look like toy buildings against big green and yellow fields.

The fields spread around engulfing towns like a whirl-pool swallows up a log while the road looks like a slow moving river rolling onwards towards Highgate and Goldthorpe.

The fields wave to and fro up hills and down low valleys. Partridges and pheasants, hares and rabbits and even foxes roam these fields.

But towns are fast growing and soon they will replace the vast fields and spreading woodlands.

The Power station at Mexborough looks like an enormous battery of guns piping shells and smoke skywards."

There have also been changes in the way spelling is dealt with and it may be helpful to consider the views of some teachers whose pupils have achieved considerable success in it.

Those teachers whose pupils' work is quoted in the last chapter nearly all agree that spelling should be taught incidentally, and that, if good reading books are plentiful and well used and writing is attacked with zest, good spelling will follow. Above all, they require a rich and plentiful supply of good individual reading books.

The following quotations indicate the way in which spelling problems are now being tackled in their schools —

(a) "Teaching of spelling and learning lists of words does not seem to help the bad speller. Generally speaking, the voracious reader spells well. We try and help the younger and less able child by means of personal dictionaries or group dictionaries.

We teach the common spelling rules and the poor reader is helped in his spelling by a phonic approach. Most of the teaching of spelling takes place incidentally. On the whole, we find that as children gain confidence in writing good spelling follows."

(b) "Sentence structure and spelling demand real effort from the child and planning by the teacher. When examining a piece of work teachers collect the most common errors which occur there, list them and have a short session with the whole class. Groups of interesting words which arise from any topic are listed and examined. Particularly in the first year and with the less-able children words are studied in their family groups.

Here, too, use is made of picture dictionaries compiled by the children."

(*c*) "Each child has a spelling book in which the teacher writes words at the child's request. Simple dictionaries are used by the junior children and reference sheets of words connected with specific topics are made easily available to the children.

Though oral vocabulary work may precede written work, lists of words are rarely left on the blackboard during the writing period as this seems not to encourage discrimination."

(*d*) "From an early age the girls use dictionaries. In the third and fourth years every child has a dictionary besides building up a personal vocabulary book. Indeed, the girls become so familiar with dictionaries that these books have now become exciting storehouses of words rather than books containing dull, monotonous lists. In this way spelling is learned naturally by the children and from the reading punctuation becomes increasingly familiar."

(*e*) "Every child is taught phonetic spelling and word building, but again rules and exceptions are learned from the reading and their desire to spell correctly in their own work. There are no exercises in learning to spell words not associated with their experiences."

(*f*) "The child who has an appetite for reading and has frequent practice in writing his own language needs little formal instruction in the complexities of English spelling. He lives with words. He knows just what they look like, he has seen them so often. He spells naturally, almost intuitively.

The reading child sees punctuation often enough. He knows where a sentence begins and ends "by ear". He sees punctuation as a necessary adjunct to expression and not as a series of esoteric tricks designed to make his English even harder for him."

(*g*) "It was realised that there was no one way which made it possible for all children to assimilate correct spelling.

Many children could spell well because of their wide reading, many needed oral aid. So much wrong spelling was the result of incorrect pronunciation. Because of this much time was spent on oral work, especially in various forms of discussion — individual at lunch-time and break-time, group and class discussion in number discovery, etc. Wide reading was encouraged, every child in the school taking home books and bringing books from home to school.

Our language is far more phonetic than we give it credit for, so after the 'whole sentence approach' followed by the 'whole word', we always watched for the correct time at which to introduce children to phonetic spelling. In this way much word building was done.

Incorrect spelling in a great number of cases was found to have arisen where poor basic teaching had allowed bad habits to develop."

(h) "Spelling is dealt with in much the same way as the errors in grammar. The child's attention is drawn to words he has mis-spelt. If the number of errors is excessive the child is made to realise this. If the child is a 'poor speller', then every encouragement is given to him if he attempts a difficult word but spells it wrongly. Only a few words are corrected at a time and these are not re-written. We find that, as a child becomes interested in what he writes, and how he writes it, he concerns himself with the words he uses, and how he spells them. All through the school the child is allowed to use a trial paper, on which he can attempt a word and take the word to his teacher for verification. He is not encouraged to take a piece of paper for a word without first having tried the word himself. In the first and second years 'Word Books' are compiled by the children which lead on in the third and fourth year to use of dictionaries, which are extensively employed at this time whenever written work is undertaken."

(i) "We acknowledge (a) that spelling is a difficulty for both young and old and (b) that the spelling of the English language is rather peculiar. Accordingly, together we learn the basic rules as quickly as possible. We have a look at word-endings and in so doing discover that bad speech is mainly to blame for our bad spelling. We try to remember this at all times and when we do this the common, local spelling errors tend to disappear. The attitude of the whole staff is vastly important. No one is expected to accept standards of speech or spelling lower than those adopted by the school. When the girls see that the teachers really care about the speech, the spelling and the quality of the written English, then the effort is made to reach the standards required. The girls know when we care and when we really mean what we say.

We do use the occasional aid to spelling because the girls like a Spelling Bee and the chance to write a playlet on the lines of the set play about the French boy trying to pronounce the words ending in 'ough'."

Whether the changes for good, to which reference has just been made and which are exemplified in Chapter III, are to continue will depend to a very great extent on whether the pressures exerted by external examinations can be reduced or not.

The next chapter discusses the nature of these examinations, and Chapter VI shows how their pressures are exerted.

Chapter V

EXTERNAL EXAMINATIONS

A. N. Whitehead in his "Aims of Education" says "no educational system is possible unless every question directly asked of a pupil at any examination is either framed or modified by the actual teacher of that pupil in that subject".

This principle is observed, or partly observed, in public examinations in other countries — at the Grammar school entrance and leaving examinations in Germany, for instance. It obtains to some extent in our training college examinations in this country.

In most of our great external examinations, however, the principle which operates is the exact opposite of that propounded by Whitehead in that no-one even remotely associated with the teaching of a child is allowed to be in any way concerned with the questions put to him.

These two principles induce two different attitudes in the minds of the teachers who are preparing the pupils for the examinations.

Where Whitehead's principle is observed the teacher tends to respond to the fact that he is being consulted in the making of a professional judgment about his pupils' attainment and abilities, and he is less likely to seek to delude himself by grooming a pupil to perform beyond his normal capacity at a given examination.

When, however, a child is being examined by an agency external to the school, the schoolmaster pits his skill against that of the external examiner and the more pupils he can get through, whatever their ability, the better the job he has done in the eyes of the pupils and parents and even of his Head and colleagues.

The Whitehead examination is part and parcel of a teacher's educational scheme and because of this he tends to rely on his own teaching material or on the few textbooks which will further the teaching aims which are his.

The external examination, however, produces an enormous superstructure of textbooks and teaching aids designed to help the classroom teacher to get his pupils through someone else's examination, an achievement which, owing to external pressures, may well have become the main object of his teaching.

Furthermore, the made-to-measure Whitehead examination is fashioned to the minds and stages of development of a handful of pupils and to further the educational aim which the teacher has for them. The reach-me-down external examination is mechanically contrived to enable a pass/fail line to be drawn on the results of tests whose main requirement is that they can be applied to tens of thousands of pupils and be objectively marked.

As Matthew Arnold once said "in this matter of mechanical contrivances the teacher will in the end always defeat us".

A brief look at examination questions set at 11+ will reveal just how far the "mechanisation" of this examination has gone.

The following questions 1 to 6 are typical of *11+ English tests*.

(1) In each of the following questions underline the word which rhymes best with the word in capital letters —

>   FLEECE   squeeze   tease   fleas   niece
>
>   GUILE   tall   oil   isle   fuel
>
>   LOUD   prude   sound   owed   proud.

(2) In the next two questions underline in the brackets the word which makes the best sense —

>   The man who performed the operation was a (doctor, nurse, anaesthetist, surgeon).
>
>   The man mending the water pipe was a (mechanic, engineer, plumber, joiner).

(3) Underline one word in each of the following sentences which ought to begin with a capital letter but does not —

>We saw johnny at the fair.
>I shall go to wales on Tuesday.
>My birthday is on february 23rd.

(4) Fill in the missing letters —

>The ship was in the h . . b . . r.
>The t . . l . r made him his suit.
>The surgeon performed the op . . . t . . n.

(5) Underline the word which most nearly means the opposite of the word in capital letters —

>NOISE   silence   bang   solemn   loud
>CHEERFUL   glad   ridiculous   sad   laughing
>SOBER   sad   comic   drunk   thrifty.

(6) Write in the blank space the correct word formed from the word in capital letters —

>DEPART   The .... of the plane is timed for 3 o'clock.
>SIGN   He put his .... at the foot of the letter.
>JUDGE   According to the .... of the court he was guilty.

Questions 7, 8 and 9 are taken from Joint Board "O" level papers.

(7) Write out in full all the *subordinate* clauses in the following passage, giving the kind, or grammatical description, and the function of each clause —

>For our torpedo trials we went up to the top of Loch Long where the formation of the hills has made an ideal stretch of water. All I had to do was to fire off the practice torpedoes. As soon as the anchor was down at the end of each run, I went ashore; I had a private arrangement with the torpedo officer that he would fly a blue flag to indicate when the next salvo was ready for firing.

(8)   Leaving childhood behind, I soon lost this desire to possess a goldfish. It is difficult to persuade oneself that a goldfish is happy and as soon as we have begun to doubt that some poor creature enjoys living with us we can take no pleasure in its company.

Using a new line for each, select *one* example from the above passage of *each* of the following —

    (*i*)   an infinitive used as the direct object of a verb;
    (*ii*)   an infinitive used in apposition to a pronoun;
    (*iii*)   a gerund;
    (*iv*)   a present participle;
    (*v*)   a past participle;
    (*vi*)   an adjective used predicatively (i.e. as a complement);
    (*vii*)   a possessive adjective;
    (*viii*)   a demonstrative adjective;
    (*ix*)   a reflexive pronoun;
    (*x*)   an adverb of time;
    (*xi*)   an adverb of degree;
    (*xii*)   a preposition;
    (*xiii*)   a subordinating conjunction.

(9)   (*a*) Construct *four* separate sentences, each sentence to include a different subordinate clause as indicated below. Underline each subordinate clause, and state its kind and function.

    (*i*)   A subordinate noun clause in apposition introduced by "that".
    (*ii*)   A subordinate adverb clause of result introduced by "that".
    (*iii*)   A subordinate noun clause as subject introduced by "that".
    (*iv*)   A subordinate adverb clause of purpose introduced by "that".

(*b*) By means of *five* short sentences, numbered correctly, give *one* example of the use of *each* of the following words, and underline your example —

    (*i*)   *After* as a preposition.
    (*ii*)   *After* as an adverb.

(iii) *After* as a subordinating conjunction.
(iv) *As* as a relative pronoun.
(v) *As* as an adverb of degree.

Note Question 7 taken from English Language Paper A   June 1956
Question 8 taken from English Language Paper A   Summer 1962
Question 9 taken from English Language Paper A   Summer 1961

Questions 10 and 11 are taken from the *N.U.J.M.B. Experimental Test in English* set in October 1962.

(10) In each of Questions 5.1 to 5.15 you are given a sentence with one word omitted, and you have to supply the missing word. Three clues are given. First, the sentence provides a context into which the word must fit. Secondly, the meaning of the word is approximately indicated by the word or phrase in brackets. Thirdly, some of the letters of the word required are given, the omission of letters being indicated by dots; the number of letters omitted is not necessarily the same as the number of dots.

In each of Questions 5.1 to 5.15, write in full, on the dotted line at the right of the page, the word required to complete the sentence.

5.1 If you are to come to your own conclusion, you must have a......s to the facts.   ....
(a way of approach)

5.2 No good workman likes to bo...... a job.   ....
(bungle)

5.3 From aid to under-developed countries, great benefits to the inhabitants will ac......e.   ....
(grow as a result)

5.4 Her beauty and charm c......te her audience.   ....
(enslave, fascinate)

etc.

(11) In each of Questions 5.16 to 5.30 you are given a sentence with either one or two words missing. After the incomplete

sentence five ways of completing it by one or two words are given; they are indicated by the letters A, B, C, D and E. You are to say which of these five words or pairs of words, when inserted in the sentence, best fits in with the meaning of the sentence as a whole. Do this by writing one of the letters A to E on the dotted line at the right of the page.

5.16 The .... of the heavens, with their periodic regularities, gave men their first .... of natural law.

    A understanding .... disproof
    B motions .... scepticism
    C chaos .... certainty
    D scrutiny .... repeal
    E contemplation .... conceptions.   ....

5.17 Let us cease to .... and instead discuss our differences without ....
    A differ .... unanimity
    B disagree .... debate
    C shadow-box .... restraint
    D squabble .... moderation
    E wrangle .... acrimony.   ....

In relation to these questions it must in fairness be said that much thought is at the present time being given to the examinations in English at the "O" and "A" level of the General Certificate, that those who are deliberating on the new Certificate of Secondary Education have high hopes that ways of examining may be devised which are helpful rather than harmful to the teaching of the subject, and that those who have produced the "Use of English" papers believe profoundly in the value of the type of questions which they are using. It is also an inescapable fact that this country is committed to examinations right through the educational system and, therefore, the only hope of improving the teaching which prepares for them is to study the harm that they do and amend them accordingly.

Unfortunately, it is not the examinations themselves which are so harmful but the time-consuming drills and exercises to which they give rise. It is probably true to say that everyone who has ever devised a major external examination believed that he was doing good, and that no-one who did so ever fully foresaw the effects of what he was creating or the uses to which it would be put.

It would be interesting to know whether those who devised the Certificate of Secondary Education and the "Use of English" papers realised that books of exercises at which children would work in preparation for these examinations would be on the market months before the first papers in them were set.

The next chapter describes the English exercises which are produced in order to help pupils to answer the type of questions which have been listed. These exercises undoubtedly constitute a major part of English teaching in the schools of the County at the present time and very great sums of money are spent each year on the production and purchase of them.

Chapter VI

ENGLISH EXERCISES

The following two passages were written by two boys whose birthdays are separated by 100 years. They are great grandfather and great grandson.

"Ashley Bridge
March 16th 1863.

The Atmosphere

Dear Sir,

The atmosphere is the air which surrounds the earth with all the various vapours. It sustains the life of man and beasts and is in fact the substance of all the whole creation. The weight of the atmosphere on the body of a man is fifteen hundred pounds on every square inch and as the body contains upon an average fifteen square feet of surface he must sustain the weight of 32,400 pounds or sixteen tons for his usual load. By this enormous pressure we should be soon crushed to atoms but for our bodies containing air or some elastic fluid. The higher we ascend in the air . . ."

"5.5.1963.

Coventry Cathedral

Homework

St. Michael's Cathedral, Coventry, was bombed terribly during the war. Only the tower remained. Thus Coventry needed a new cathedral and in 1947 a reconstruction committee was formed headed by the bishop.

To choose an architect a competition was held and the winner was Sir Basil Spence.

He designed the cathedral and with the committee's approval chose the people to work on it.

Gradually the cathedral grew and it was at last officially opened in 1962 after at least 8 years' work. Every part of the new cathedral is modern and in an entirely different style from other English cathedrals.

When I visited it, the parts which I liked best were the windows, especially the Piper baptistry window which is especially designed . . ."

The boy who wrote the first passage was born in 1850; he was the son of a Lancashire weaver who attended the local British school first as a pupil and later as a pupil teacher. He was awarded a Queen's Scholarship to the Borough Road College and it may, therefore, be presumed that he was in modern terms a good sixth-former who would today easily get to the University. He was 13 when he wrote the passage quoted.

His great grandson, born a hundred years later in 1950 and a pupil at a West Riding Comprehensive school, wrote his passage after a visit to Coventry Cathedral when he too was 13. He will be taking his G.C.E. in at least eight "O" levels just before he is 16 years of age. The two boys may, therefore, be considered similar in native ability.

It may be profitable to compare the teaching which led to these two pieces of work.

The school programme of the first boy consisted of Arithmetic, Object lessons, History, Geography and Scripture. It appears that he spent a considerable amount of time at home and at school in the exercise of parsing.

It might be considered that the first boy's writing shows greater erudition than that of his great grandson, but it is doubtful whether it shows greater facility of expression and, in any case, it must not be forgotten that the great grandson in the same amount of time available for his studies reaches a good standard in Latin, French, Physics, Chemistry, Biology, Mathematics, Art and Woodwork, none of which was studied by his great grandfather.

But the interesting thing is the time spent on parsing. The first boy when he was 12 in 1862 wrote this —

| As | conjunction |
| a | adj lim. man |

man	com. noun mas gen 3 per sing num, non case to "lives"
lives	reg. intran. verb ind. mood pres. ten 3 per sing num agrees with man
so	adverb of manner
will	aux. of tense den. the future
he	per. pron mas gen 3 per sing num nom case of will die
die	reg. intran. verb indic. mood fut. tense 3 per sing num.

Two years earlier, when he was ten, he spent much time parsing sentences such as "Truth lies at the bottom of a well", "Before the bright sun rises o'er the hill", "Vice lives and thrives in concealment", and "I doubt if he who lolls his head where idleness and plenty meet, enjoys his pillow or his bread as those who earn the meals they eat".

The first boy must have spent many hundreds of hours in his life parsing in this way and he did so, quite clearly, for one reason only — that it was firmly believed by those who taught him that if he did not perform this exercise he would never learn to write English well.

His great grandson, when questioned, said he was not quite sure whether he had ever done any parsing; he thought he did some "in Latin" two years ago. But it is certain that few, if any, of the children whose work is quoted in this book have ever done parsing as an exercise.

It is difficult to escape the conclusion that a vast amount of the time our gradfathers spent on this exercise was educational folly of a high order. Their doing so was based on the assumption that if a child can take someone else's sentences to pieces and label the parts he will write better ones of his own. It is as sensible to believe that a man who curses his mate's clumsiness will do so the better if he knows that the word he is using is an "expletive".

The extraordinary thing about this is that almost everyone who has ever done any sixth form French will remember this conversation — "Quoi! quand je dis 'Nicole apportez-moi mes pantoufles et me

donnez mon bonnet de nuit' c'est de la prose. 'Oui, Monsieur.'
Par ma foi il y a plus de quarante ans que je dis de la prose sans
que j'en susse rien." The answer of Nicole the serving maid when all
this is explained to her is to the point. It may roughly be translated
"and where does all this get you?"

The important question which follows from all this is, what in our
day is replacing the parsing that our grandfathers did?

The answer in some schools, of course, is parsing, but in the main
we do exercises from books which sell in millions and are bought
forty at a time by thousands of schools. The industry is a vast and,
no doubt, a most lucrative one.

It is possible that some of these exercises may be helpful to
children's learning, but it is significant that nearly all the schools
from which the quoted examples are drawn either do not use them
because they have no need to do so or deliberately avoid their use as
being harmful to the learning process.

As has already been said, an impressive collection of these books
used in the home has been made by people walking into shops and
asking "Have you an English book which will help a child to get
through his scholarship?" A much more comprehensive collection
of school books can be made by a perusal of catalogues or by walking
into the supplies department of a large Local Authority.

Many of these books consist of collections of general knowledge
questions aimed at children of a certain age such as —

> What do we call a mermaid's father?
> What do we call the home of a horse?
> What do we call someone who sells fish?

In many there are collected together exercises which can perhaps
best be described as "gimmicks". For example, a child may be asked
to "build a tower" starting with the letter "i" and the child is
expected to write —

i	or	i
it		in
lit		pin
slit		pine
slits		spine.

A list of jumbled letters may be given and the child asked to re-write them as boys' names. For example —

MOTYM	HONYJN
REEPT	CLAE.

A list of letters may be given and the child asked to form them into the names of three animals. For example —

WOODGGPIC

A sentence may be given and the child required to make a word out of the initial letter of each word in it. For example —

Take the first letter of each word in the following sentence and make a word which means a form of writing —

"Some enter popular old restaurants."

If questions of this kind were included in a collection which is intended to prepare pupils for a so-called "intelligence" test, there might be some excuse for them, as there seems to be no limit to the oddness of questions asked in such tests, but it is extremely difficult to believe that they will in fact make children write more fluently and expressively.

Other questions to be found in books of exercises consist of blank-filling, such as —

Complete the following —

Night is to Day as Moon is to ....

Cow is to Milk as Hen is to ....

Horse is to Foal as Cat is to ....

Some deliberately put down wrong spellings which have to be corrected —

Don't shout when in dout.

When I'm busy I like a drink that's fusy.

He saw a solissiter talking to a theif.

Some aim at spelling —

Add "ing" to smile, fulfil, enjoy, go.

Add "ei" or "ie" to br . . f, rel . . f, s . . ve.

Many of the questions demand underlining only —

Underline the word which means almost the same as the word in capital letters —

EXACT	similar	precise	complete	alike
GRATITUDE	pleasure	delight	thankfulness	happy.

In almost all these books there are a number of comprehension exercises consisting of a piece of prose on which questions are asked. It is an interesting commentary on these questions that a class of senior boys who were engaged in "comprehension", and had in fact been heading their work each week for four years by this word, did not know its meaning when asked by a visitor to the school.

The books aimed at the Grammar school pupil are most of them directed at formal questions on English Grammar.

They include comprehension exercises, which, of course, can be valuable, but pupils may be asked to make up examples of synecdoche or litotes, meiosis or metaphor. More common is the question aimed at sentence analysis. The pupil may be given a piece of prose and asked to write out the clauses in it, stating their grammatical function, or he may have to illustrate clauses of various kinds introduced by words which are given to him such as "an adverbial clause of purpose introduced by 'lest'".

Other questions aim more directly still at grammatical analysis and require the pupil to use a present participle as a subject of a verb or a present participle used as an adjective or a parenthetical infinitive phrase or a gerund as the subject of a verb.

To many teachers the "Use of English" paper contrived by the Universities is a disturbing development. Clearly, the Universities are dissatisfied with the results of the kind of teaching which their influence has brought about in the schools over the last 30 years. Whether their newer techniques, which make full use of blank-filling and underlining, will improve matters remains to be seen.

The following extracts from reviews of books of exercises illustrate quite clearly what kind of books they are and what they are intended to do —

1. "The questions are of the type set in the 11+ English paper that is used by many L.E.A's."
2. "In the exercises on each topic the tradional plurals, jumbled words, rhyming words, small examples of description, completion of sentences, and so on, are presented with more simple illustrations."
3. "There are about 40 sets of exercises in each book to allow a week's work in each."

4. "An unusual and splendid feature of these books is the 30 pages of English language tests in Book 5 to assess a child's attainment in English at the promotion stage."

5. "The teaching is effected through comprehensive lists of the various parts of speech, antonyms, synonyms, similes, idioms, proverbs, which can be used both for memorisation and for reference.
The book can be used to teach . . . explanations are given of language facts and rules . . . and to test."

6. "The section comprises capital letters, better-best, the apostrophe 's', question and answer, is-his and as-has, is-are, inverted commas, have-has, say-says, am-is-are, where-were, was-were, did-done, . . ."

Unless some determined study is made to see if these exercises have any real value in English teaching, it seems that not only will they continue but will greatly increase. Books designed to prepare pupils for a Certificate of Secondary Education examination are already on the market, and no doubt next year sixth-formers will be busy working through "Use of English" preparation books containing such questions as "Name a word meaning officialdom which ends in ......cracy".

Indeed "University Entrance Tests in the Use of English" have already been published and of one book it is said by the publisher — "This book is designed to meet the needs of the 'Use of English' examination which all University candidates must pass. It provides stimulating material for free composition and comment as well as plenty of exercises of the more routine kind. Fifteen full-length papers are provided: they are all different in form, as it is one of the aims not to make this examination stereotyped."

One might perhaps ask — "How many books of exercises does it require to stereotype an examination?"

If the teachers who use these books of exercises are satisfied that their pupils produce better English than that quoted in Chapter III, well and good; if they are not, they would do well to reflect on the fact that the teachers who produced the work in Chapter III from the Infant to the Grammar schools make little or no use of them.

CONCLUSION

This short book has been concerned with the main tool of learning. Many children, particularly those in the industrial areas of the country, start their educational lives at the age of five with this tool blunt, and live their early years in home circumstances which often conspire to keep it blunt, with the result, as the young sixth-former wrote in Chapter I, that even he "becomes increasingly conscious of his inadequate vocabulary, lack of fluency and lazy, slovenly speech", which may become "the most prominent manifestation of his embarrassment and discomfort".

To avoid this, to give the child the confidence which derives from ease of speech and writing, is surely one of the prime tasks of the schools of the County.

There is no single recipe for a way to do this well, but it may be helpful to consider the conditions which appear to be common to the Primary schools whose work has been quoted.

In all of them the Head is much more readily excited by how children learn than by what they learn. In all, respect for the children as individuals is such that few problems of discipline arise in the schools. Most of the schools from which work was taken are unstreamed, but it would be wrong to infer that this fact of organisation resulted in good written English; rather is it true to say that the same attitude in Head and staff which led to unstreaming also produced the English.

In all the schools from which the work was taken a wide range of individual reading books of high quality has replaced the old class reader, and great care is given to the quality of literature read to the pupils. Very little, if any, use is made in these schools of books of English exercises, and in all of them there is a lively and enlightened interest in other media of expression in art, clay, movement and fabric. Indeed, a number of the Heads have gone out of their way to say how firmly convinced they are that success in one medium encourages and supports success in another.

All the schools lay the very greatest importance on the value of first-hand experience as a means of stimulating good written work. But they insist that the experience must be appropriate to the stage of development of the child to whom it is offered. It must be well planned and wisely and thoroughly followed up in reading and further investigation.

In most of the Primary schools it is notable that children are given a period each day in which they select what they wish to do from a variety of activities, and it is often in those activity periods that some of the best written work is done.

Correcting is done in a way which does not inhibit the flow of expression, and in the stimulation of work every possible effort is made to praise what is good rather than condemn failure. Techniques such as spelling and punctuation are for the most part taught incidentally to individual children when the child's work is being read and enjoyed.

Good "personal" writing is something which comes slowly to a school and is the result of many subtle forces and influences working within it. What is written is a by-product of these forces, the product being the developing children themselves. So much is this so that one would doubt the value and sincerity of any quick results, as it is unfortunately all too true that a teacher determined to get results can make a child produce almost anything from "abstract art" to poetry. Indeed, one of the dangers of publishing work such as is set out in this book is that it may be copied or become "the thing to do".

However, perhaps the most striking thing about all the schools quoted is that they are happy, active, well-kept places from which zest and eagerness in staff and pupils seem to have dispelled problems of control and discipline.

Much of what has been said about the Primary schools would obtain in the Secondary schools too, but more particularly in the relationship between the Head, the teacher of English, and the pupils. It may also, but would not necessarily, apply in the teaching of other specialist subjects.

The purpose in compiling this book is not to condemn external examinations, the use of English exercises, or the wise teaching of English grammar. Indeed, in the acquisition of almost any skill there is a time for drills and exercises and this almost always comes at the moment when the learner himself is urgently aware of the need for it. Neither is it intended to suggest that there is no place for "English" in the Secondary school time-table or for the sound use of comprehension tests.

The main point of the book is to give rise to discussion, not only amongst teachers of English, but amongst Heads and, indeed, all teachers who use English as the means of communicating and recording in the subjects which they teach — the geographer, historian, scientist, and so on. The questions to be discussed are many and varied.

(a) What should be the main aim of the teaching of English?

(b) Is it true that one learns to write by writing?

(c) Should "English Language" as such exist as a subject in its own right?

(d) Does its existence as a subject tend to lessen the responsibility of other subject teachers for the quality of the language used in their subject?

(e) How much grammar should be taught to able children at the Junior and Secondary stages, and how much to slow learners?

(f) How are spelling and punctuation best taught?

(g) What are the best ways of enriching a child's vocabulary?

(h) If the main purpose of teaching English Language is to enable children to express themselves clearly, how is it possible for pupils in their "O" level Literature paper to score very high marks indeed and yet to score low ones, or even fail, in the English Language paper?

But perhaps the main facts to be weighed and considered are that most of the work quoted in this book is by pupils who have known little of formal grammar or the English exercises, which are the mainstay of so much English teaching. Indeed, it is to be doubted whether work of this quality could be produced by schools in which English teaching consisted mainly of English exercises, yet so prevalent is this method that many a Secondary school pupil believes he is being ill-taught if he is not subjected to it. Moreover, it must be admitted that most of the teachers who teach English by using comprehension tests and grammatical and other exercises do so because they know no other way of teaching it.

However this may be, a teacher who has come to rely excessively on such exercises would be ill-advised suddenly to abandon them because another teacher can teach well without them. He would do better first of all quietly and patiently to consider why he is teaching in the way he is teaching and whether his teaching is producing work of quality. If his answers to these questions are unconvincing, he should begin gradually to experiment and change his ways.

Perhaps it would be a good thing if all Heads of schools, together with the members of their staffs concerned in one way or another with the writing and speaking of English, considered the following remark made by a teacher of English in a West Riding Grammar school —

> ". . . What nonsense it is to take 'English Language' as a subject at any time or stage. Better by far have children-conscious, language-conscious teachers doing no end of things with children and what's written up or talked about is 'English'."

APPENDIX

Statement by a boy, in his first year in the sixth form of a South Yorkshire Grammar school, on the effect of social pressures on speech and language.

"The problem of speech facing a sixth former in a working class area is only a relatively minor one. It is a reflection of the much greater complexities he faces in having to live two lives, but his speech may be the most prominent manifestation of his embarrassment and discomfort. He is conscious always of being different. He has received an education that does not permit him to accept the values and general habits of his friends and relatives. He cannot yet, however, feel part of the sort of life he is being pushed into and feels conscious of his social background when in the company of well-spoken middle-class children. Of course, again, the main cause of this discomfort is lack of communication.

A child goes to a grammar school completely unaware that forces will be set to play on him which will force a division between himself and his parents and the world from which he came. He is unaware that in later years he will assume a privileged position and (for good or ill) will feel superior to his counterparts not receiving higher education. He is unaware also of the great difficulties he will encounter when he later finds himself alone and cut off from all ties to the real world and when he ensconces himself in a secluded academic world of his own. These changes are not significant until he reaches the sixth form. At this stage the narrow academic life hitherto led makes itself felt on his personality as he matures into a young man. This young man has neither confidence, social ease nor fluent speech but within two years he will enter the adult world of the University. The sixth-former is thus a hybrid of a working class child and an educated middle-class child.

As the sixth-former becomes increasingly conscious of his inadequate vocabulary, lack of fluency and lazy, slovenly speech (accent is unimportant), he may attempt to do something about it, but his normal social environment is not conducive to good speech nor to the standard of social etiquette he is expected to acquire. Moreover, the effect of his trying to speak 'the Queen's English' the effect may be ludicrous and create the wrong impression. When speaking in his usual surroundings too he may be ridiculed and he feels that he is despised. People use such an opportunity as an excuse to deride someone of whose success they are jealous and who represents to them the personification of the traditional enemy of the working class.

As he ascends each rung of the educational ladder, through various strata in the class hierarchy he leaves behind the life he has known and feels increasingly embarrassed and confused. Some may adjust, but many find the strain too much and never leave the life they know and may leave school but do not distinguish themselves in examinations.

Such are the emotional stresses experienced by a working class sixth-former that his personality may be permanently harmed. He may become an introvert and develop an inferiority complex for which he may over-compensate and so create an unpleasant impression. Further, there may be a tendency to assume an air of superiority at home to compensate for distress at school and later at University.

By the time he reaches the sixth-form he has been so far indoctrinated that his one purpose in life is 'to get on' (Where to? — it may not occur to him to ask himself). Moreover, 'to get on' means interviews, speeches and many social occasions which demand well-bred manners, social ease and good speech. In order to avoid 'sitting still with thumb in mouth and fumbling fingers' at his University interview he may eventually decide to make a concerted effort to be master in his own house and to correct his speech. Such a course frequently causes friction in his family and amongst acquaintances when he finds himself inadvertently correcting their speech. As he becomes a better speaker he becomes increasingly annoyed at those who don't. Education in general has made him incompatible with working-class life.

The problem could be a temporary one. Universal Comprehensive Secondary Education could remove the paradoxical situation of educated children and uneducated parents. It has been found that greater class mobility by means of a Selective Secondary education is necessary for the continued existence of our country by utilising our sole natural resource — our Brains. Little thought has been spared, however, to the strains and stresses undergone by children forced between various strata of society. Until education is considered as a social problem rather than in economic terms and until a more enlightened educational policy along these lines is pursued the situation will be perpetuated, with all sorts of repercussions."